SHINIWA

The Story of a Reclaimed Life

An Autobiography by

Michael La Vasani

Order this book online at www.trafford.com
or email orders@trafford.com

Most Trafford titles are also available at major online book retailers.

Printed in the United States of America.

ISBN: 978-1-4269-2082-0 (sc)
ISBN: 978-1-4269-2083-7 (hc)

Library of Congress Control Number: 2009939889

Trafford rev. 06/14/2012

Trafford
PUBLISHING® www.trafford.com

North America & international
toll-free: 1 888 232 4444 (USA & Canada)
phone: 250 383 6864 ♦ fax: 812 355 4082

To My Daughter
Melody C. La Vasani

CONTENTS

PART V

HOW SHINIWA CAME TO BE

ADMITTEDLY THIS STORY IS STRANGE ALMOST BEYOND belief. It is very real, however, because I lived it and survived it through the patient determination of a Buddhist monk who never gave up on a lost boy filled with rage and hatred.

The original purpose in writing down this account was as a wedding gift to my beloved child, Melody, who grew up not knowing any of these details. I was determined to make her life as beautiful as mine had been ghastly.

Several things occurred to me in the process of writing down all these memories that gave me other reasons to continue putting down on paper events that are almost too painful to recall.

For the memory of my angelic sister, Shahla, who died a cruel death to cancer, I happily dedicate proceeds of my story to research and treatment of children with that dread disease.

For parents, this is a story that should be a clarion call to think how your behavior can destroy the life of a child. If my story can prevent even one father or mother from becoming an abusive alcoholic, it is worth all the pain of writing it down.

The real story belongs to a saintly Buddhist monk who gave me the name of Shiniwa, the rising sun, when I was more like the fiercest cyclone. That godly monk will always represent to me the very epitome of love, which was a rare commodity in my early years.

His love for me had nothing to do with any kind of proselytizing to make me believe anything other than the goodness that was in me, no matter how deeply buried.

Reading the story of this work on my very soul, is a kind of enlightenment leading to a life of calm and serenity. A child as distorted by cruelty and hate as I had been is most likely, in our harried civilization, to be thrown into the garbage heap and forgotten.

Perhaps the transformation that happened to me is yet another reason for telling my story. It is a roadmap to a better existence, showing how love and patience really can reclaim a life. So I invite one and all to travel with me from despair to equanimity and, like me, one day ask the question . . .

EPILOGUE

IN 2003, I TRAVELED BACK TO WHERE I HAD STARTED MY hike to the monastery that became my house for almost eleven years. I could not find my way around through all the newer constructions or massive beltway pavements. The small fishing village had disappeared and a moderate size industrial city had replaced it.

Although, I had always called the second monastery as Luery, I learnt that it only meant "a second home" in local language. I spent many days in the search of the old trails to the monastery. Everything looked different. Han Chinese constituted more than 90% of the city population. I felt the strong presence of unwelcome Chinese occupation of a land that had fought the Communist Regime for almost fifty years at the cost of thousands of innocent young lives.

China declared that when it invaded the isolated kingdom of Tibet in 1950, it brought modernity and respected the nominal autonomy of the centuries old feudal theocracy. Within the decade, that proved to be cruel fiction.

The beautiful land suffered disastrously from the extremism of Chinese politics in the 1960s. Many died in work camps while hundreds of monasteries were destroyed. Chinese brutal occupation of the most isolated nation on earth has sealed the fate of its centuries old theocracy.

I met an old monk who had heard about the footballer monks. He told me that Chinese had invaded and destroyed both monasteries. The monks fate who were imprisoned in Chinese labor camps were unknown.

I was shocked. Our monastery was inside Nepal border while Luery was hardly located within Tibet territory.

PRELUDE

TWO MEN SAT IN THE SEMI-DARKNESS OF THE PALATIAL library. The atmosphere between them smelled of tension and unspeakable fear, though the younger of the two seemed almost pleased in the way of a cat that has just dined on the canary.

He spoke, "It's finished. You're finally rid of the demon you spawned. They have taken him far into the mountains in that no-man's land between China, Nepal, and India. If he survives the trip on foot, he won't survive the political unrest, Chinese occupation of Tibet and harsh conditions of Himalayas. He will not endure the tensions, as I am sure he will get himself killed. I deem that our Chinese friends will take care of our little problem. There is no place for him to run. It's far too isolated. Even if he tries, he will not survive."

There was a brief silence as the boy's father lifted his bottle of imported Scotch whisky to his lips and stared into the darkness in his usual alcoholic stupor.

His brother continued, "In a few years, you can announce that the boy is dead. Everyone knows he was sent away to school where his sister died tragically. You can just say he was killed in an auto accident, or fell into the river, or whatever demise you think up for him. No one will be the wiser, and his blood will not be on your hands."

The boy's father turned his head to look at his brother, took another swig directly out of the bottle he held precariously in his hand.

"It is good," he said and closed his eyes against the truth.

I wasn't there, of course. This is just the way I always imagined the scene played out all those years ago in the house where I was born in Iran.

"How can you hate Love?"

A family is a place where minds come in contact with one another.
If these minds love one another, the home will be as beautiful as
a flower garden. But if these minds get out of harmony with one
another, it is like a storm that plays havoc with the garden

PART I

RAGE

CHAPTER ONE

MOLDING A MONSTER

THERE ARE TWO KINDS OF HEAT. ONE, OF COURSE, IS the blistering atmosphere of a Middle Eastern desert where every surface reflects the unrelenting glare of the whiteness of the sun during the mid-day. That is a type of heat that can be dealt with by retreating into a cool, dim place like the Bedouins taking shelter under their tents, or in my case, staying inside a typical Middle Eastern mansion with its cool marble floors broken up by expensive Persian rugs that came from my family's factory. In the late afternoon or evening, I might splash around in the family pool, being careful to stay in the shallow end because I had not yet learned to swim. In the air conditioned house, I could always find something cold to drink and often enjoy the cool touch of my grandmother's rough hands on my face or running her fingers through the curls on my tawny head. Grandmother was one of my refuges, an oasis of kindness and comfort I could count on when there was very little else dependable in my environment that some would call privileged.

That kind of heat was easy to deal with. The other, a live ember in the pit of my stomach, a fire in my soul, could not be escaped by any physical means. It was there constantly, searing my very being, boiling my five-year-old blood with intensity far greater than the radiant sun. At the time, I had no vocabulary to describe that heat that all but consumed me night and day. I had no label to fix onto emotions that had been a part of my very being, probably since the day I was born, because they say that infants sense things—that they know by instinct what we gradually learn by reason as we grow older. That hot coal at the core of my very being I recognize now was rage, an anger far stronger than any felt by a prisoner in a torture chamber. Unlike escaping from the blistering sun, there was no escape from the fire within.

It is something of a black comedy now to think that there were people who envied my family because of the opulence of our walled palace with its maids, butlers, gardeners, and cleaners who worked around the clock to keep the heavily guarded compound immaculate and away from the prying eyes of strangers. People whose circumstances admitted of only doing for themselves actually envied the fact that my family had underlings waiting on their every need or desire. What appeared to be a haven of refuge on the outside was actually an inferno of family dysfunction that produced the rage in my youthful heart and created in me a monster of unimaginable dimensions.

If my father was the Devil incarnate who stoked the flames of hell within our compound walls, I was the Demon in charge during his frequent absences, lashing out viciously at everyone I imagined had slighted me in the least. The difference between us was that I was not an alcoholic and my rage was reactionary whereas his behavior was sadistic and calculated. The fact that he had been an abused child when he was living at home held no water with me. If Grandmother, the only adult in the house who ever stood up to my father, wanted to make allowances for his despicable behavior, well and good; but none of her sweetness and understanding ever rubbed off on me. My rage was fuelled by the consuming hate I felt not only for my father but also for my mother who endured his brutality without fighting back, who stood wordlessly by when he abused me or my sister, who seemed only concerned about the bruises and cuts on her own body. I never once felt any love emanating from her, and that void in my young mind turned to loathing. Once, when right in front of me, my father in one of his drunken rages lifted her skirts and brutally raped her, I felt no compassion, only contempt that she did not retaliate by putting poison in his whisky or stabbing him in one of his alcoholic stupors.

Father's vast wealth and political power is incidental to my story except to point out that dysfunctional families and child abuse are not exclusive domains of the poor. While I lived in my opulent surroundings, I had no concept of what went on outside our protective walls. It was many years later before I grasped the extent of my father's political and economic power in a regime that would one day crumble under its own abuses taking him down with it. All I knew was the torment I lived with night and day and how my mode of self-preservation built up the rage within that could explode under any circumstance that caused me to feel threatened.

Looking back now, I can see how the connection my father and his younger brother, Imad, had with Shah Mohammad Reza Pahlavi played such a part in their accumulations of wealth and power. My Uncle Imad had actually been a classmate of the Shah which propelled him into power as a General of the Iranian Air Force when Pahlavi was returned to the Peacock Throne in 1941 with the aid of the American CIA. To compound my father's position of wealth and power, he married my mother, daughter of a Khan in the city of Kashan known for its exquisite Persian rugs which were produced by her family, largely with slave labor. The Khans (feudal lords) in

Iran were rich, powerful, independent, often at odds with each other and lawless—they took and did whatever they wanted with impunity. Mother was an exception for Iranian women at the time in that she was educated abroad. Her arranged marriage to my father solidified an incredible power base that he relished, wielding it effectively against all his enemies—except one—his five-year-old son.

In spite of her education, my mother, Touran Kashi La Vasani, lived like other Iranian women, totally subservient to their husbands and useful only as child bearers. At my early age, I understood nothing of her disappointment in the life she had been dealt.

To get a picture of the dynamics of how I vented my pent up rage, it is necessary to understand the physical strength of my small five-year-old frame. As the son of one of the wealthiest and most powerful men in the country, I had every toy and amusement that money could buy, but I disdained them all except my football (which Americans call a soccer ball). My football was my friend, my constant companion; and by perpetual practice with my ball I developed astonishing strength in my legs. In short, I had the kick of a mule and the bite of a tiger at a very early age, and that kick and those sharp teeth, along with a vengeful heart, were my defense mechanisms. Nor was I intimidated by threats of violence against me. Even my abusive father began to see that his maltreatment of me had no effect whatsoever and, in time, he actually came to fear my violent outbursts.

Grandmother was the only living human being safe from my rage even though there was one other family member for whom I felt something as close to love as was possible in a heart so scarred as the one that resided in the embers of my soul. That was my beautiful older sister, Shahla. She had inherited the best of both my mother and my grandmother—like our mother, she was breathtakingly beautiful, a girl who might have been chosen as a beauty queen or movie star. She resembled Mother physically, though she was even more attractive, but her beautiful temperament was that of Grandmother's, so kind and gentle, accepting her life circumstances with an equanimity that was impossible within my savage breast.

My abuse of Shahla amounted to the kind of mental cruelty I learned from Father. I called her hateful names and ordered her about like a young lord, the prerogative of males in the society into which we had been born. None of my unwarranted viciousness toward Shahla ever altered one iota of her love and devotion to me, notwithstanding the fact that I could not recognize what she gave me in the form of love that never emanated from either of our parents.

No one except grandmother was immune from my potent kick as I was not immune from my father's physical abuse, physical beatings just to prove the point that he was the head of the house, the lord and master, the arbiter of our souls. He could not really hurt me most of the time because he was too drunk to stand up. Nevertheless he left bruises and welts on my body that I bore proudly as marks of my courage.

After one of my beatings, Shahla would say things like, "Does it hurt? Do you want me to put my hand on it to keep it warm? Do you want some water? Do you want to play?" My cruel response to her solicitation usually ran something like, "Get lost, you creep." I was unaffected by seeing her sit in the corner of the room with tears gathering in her incredibly green eyes. How Shahla and Grandmother could remain so gentle in our infernal atmosphere is still something of a mystery to me. Both of them knew what was happening deep inside me, so they spent great effort in trying to make me understand, to make me love. But I was unable to love another human being, seeing them all (except for Grandmother and Shahla) as antagonists.

There were only two loves in my young life, and the first of those was my football, my constant companion that filled the void of loneliness in my life. Although I had no concept of other family dynamics, I was all too conversant with the abuse and neglect from my alcoholic father. The other children about my age in the neighborhood where we lived were not my equals, poor boys who bragged about their fathers as heroes and companions. I didn't believe them. I hated them, and we were constantly getting into fights. I gave no quarter when I fought—kicking, biting, and hurting until my rage was vented enough for them to limp away howling in pain. When their parents brought them to the house to complain, there were usually only the servants to see the damage because my parents were seldom at home. I suspect those parents knew when they came that my father would not be at home. He was not a man who was loved, but rather a man who was feared because of his wealth and political power. Everyone was terrified to confront him except his five-year-old son who had become immune to his abuses and relentless in showing his great contempt for the man who should have been the most important person in my life.

My litany of damnation toward my father was emphatic and uncompromising, a catalog of indictments he could not deny because they were all true. It should have stunned him out of his vileness, but it never did, only making him more distant and wrapped up in himself.

"You are never at home!" I accused, "Who am I to play with? You don't even know what I like to do! Do you know anything about my school? Have you ever seen my school reports? Do you know that I was throwing up all night last night? How do you think I feel when Mother says I cannot watch TV because I might wake you up out of a drunken sleep? What is my name? How old am I? Does your precious bottle let you stay sober enough to know the difference between making love to my mother and raping her? What are those scars on her right arm? Do you remember the day you almost killed me and my sister when we were playing behind your car? Who are all those strange men who come to our house? What are they doing here? I hate you! I hate you! I hate you!"

Those were sparks from the ember that glowed painfully in my breast, but they were words never spoken. Deep inside was that glow, fanned by the flames of abuse and neglect, aggravated by a drunken bully who should have been a loving father. No, I never said those things to a father I never had. Calling him Father was a convention of biological proportions, not an endearment from a hero worshiping son like the boys in the neighborhood I envied so much that I could only inflict injury and pain on their proud faces.

If my invective seemed advanced for my tender years, I was later tested and evaluated to have a MENSA level IQ at a very early age. Perhaps the slings and arrows of dysfunctional family life would not have enraged me so had I not possessed that intelligence without the benefit of physical maturity. Who knows? It is fair to say that home environment juxtaposed with the cultural preferential treatment of a male heir worked together to create the monster I became. Like my role model, I enjoyed inflicting pain, both physical and mental, on anyone who crossed my path. The one exception, however, was Grandmother, a woman of such character and dignity that not even my brute of a father could stand up to her. A woman of small stature, when she raised herself to her full height and stared sightlessly at father, he wilted like a flower left out of the vase. Had I been a little older, I would have recognized that it was not respect for Grandmother that made Father back down, it was mortal fear.

CHAPTER TWO

A SEED OF LOVE

GRANDMOTHER'S STRENGTH DID NOT COME FROM HER great wealth or physical stamina; rather it came from an innate goodness and an abiding love for me and my sister. Shahla may have understood just how much we meant to Grandmother; I only understood that she was comforting and nurturing in a way my parents never were. Her fingers were rough from all the years she spent in the rug making business, but to this day I can close my eyes and feel how pacifying those fingers were as she ran them through my curly hair. She could talk to me, though I rarely heeded her admonitions, yet I did not resent them, either.

Outside our compound on a small rise in the landscape, I played daily with my friend the football. It never occurred to me how strong my legs were growing from that constant practice of manipulating the ball with my feet. I only felt the closest thing to love I was capable of as I kicked and bounced the beloved ball for hours on end. Occasionally it got the better of me and went skipping down the small hill to collide against the wall of a small shop. The merchant would come outside shaking his fists and shouting invective every time that happened. In a heart like mine, already filled with rage, his behavior only fanned the flame of revenge within my core, heating up that ember that was constantly just below the surface.

What began as an accident of the ball getting out of my control then became an all out war with my deliberate slams of the ball against his shop wall or the glass window in front. I actually felt pleasure out of seeing him lose his cool. He was an obese man which made his fist waving threats even funnier to me, and I began calling him Fat Man as an insult. On occasion when Father happened to be passing by his shop, Fat Man would come out and complain bitterly about me, suggesting that one day I would end up on the gallows. When he talked, his jowls jiggled and veins popped out on his forehead. He raised a fist making circular motions in the air like the propeller of a small plane. Father seemed to think the Fat Man was both over reacting and overly dramatic, but that fact did not spare me his wrath when we returned home, which only served to make me hate Fat Man even more.

Fat Man's remarks that I would end up a gangster dangling from a noose galled me, and I began planning a sweet revenge even as I continued to slam my ball against his window and laugh at his absurd posturing and venomous curses. An avenue for revenge presented itself to me one day when I came across a dead snake, a creature much feared in the deserts of the Middle East. Gleefully, I coiled the dead reptile around the handle of the front door of his shop early in the morning before he came to open up. Hidden not far away, I watched as he took out his key and inserted it into the lock. At that moment he looked down, saw the snake, and fell back in a dead faint. I could scarcely contain my laughter as I watched Fat Man being carried away by the paramedics. No one had touched the snake—it was a serpent and it was dead, a double whammy for the devout Muslims in the area.

My revenge was not complete at that point, however. The rage had not been sufficiently mollified. No one at the clinic just a block away where they took Fat Man even noticed the small boy slip inside carrying something well concealed and listening for a room number. Stealthily, I got into the room and placed the snake between the sheets of the bed where they would soon deposit my enemy. There was no way for me to remain in the clinic and witness what happened next, but it was a long time before Fat Man was seen back at his shop.

It was Grandmother who admonished me about the merchant saying, "I love you, son; you warm my heart and brighten my day. You are both the light of my darkness and my travail in life. Don't call him Fat Man." The words and her fingers in my hair soothed me as I thought about how I could be the light of her darkness. Her sightless eyes enthralled me and I said to her, "Grandmother, your eyes are so blue just like the sky." It would be years later before I really understood her response, "They are the dark blue of the night sun." Grandmother saw so much, it was difficult to think of her as being blind. There were many other things about Grandmother I failed to understand as well. Why does a woman of her wealth and position roll up her sleeves and go about helping the servants who are being paid to perform their duties? Why does Grandmother always speak softly to me without reproach when I allow my rage to vent itself on Shahla or the neighborhood boys or Fat Man? It would be many years in the future before I would come across another human being with that same kind of gentleness, compassion, and love; only then would I grasp completely the depth of Grandmother's goodness and how she was dedicated to alleviating the rage that burned within my breast. For me there was no concept of the sky ending on a note of just simple love.

CHAPTER THREE

THE WILL TO KILL

IF MY RAGE HAD BEEN BOILING UNDER THE SURFACE, IT was about to erupt with a violence that would put Vesuvius to shame. It all had to do with the one other thing in my life that I truly and dearly loved—Dookie, my pet rooster. I would come home from school and immediately start searching for Dookie, my strutting varicolored friend with the bright red cockscomb and flashing, beady eyes. Dookie who allowed me to stroke his brilliant plumage and talked his "pawk, pawk" that I imagined I could understand. Maybe I could. I knew when he was thirsty or hungry, and Dookie listened to me when I chattered out the events of my day, the hate I harbored for my father, or the imaginary games I wanted to play. Like with the football, there was never any conflict between me and my friend. Well, almost never—he took great exception when I pretended to be Zorro and attempted to ride him for my horse. I constantly tried to sit on his back and he struggled to free himself in a perpetual contest of wills that Dookie always won. I so loved that rooster that there was never any anger or resentment on my part when the attempt at riding him inevitably came to no avail. Neither did I vent my frustration at him when all my attempts to get him to eat ice cream resulted in his indignant refusal of what I considered a treat. Any human, except for Grandmother, who denied me my slightest wish was sure to feel the fury of my wrath.

Father hated Dookie, which was about the highest recommendation anyone could possible give me for bonding with my rooster as a friend. He was mine exclusively and even my beloved sister, Shahla, was not immune from my over protectiveness of Dookie.

"Can I touch him?" she asked.

"No!" I barked, "He's thirsty. Go get him some water!"

My rage and my culture caused me to order Shahla about like a scullery maid without the slightest tone of gentleness in my voice. I had no concept of behavior other than acting out from the only role model I had ever known, my father, the dictatorial brute, the king of the dysfunctional family. Perhaps, I wondered later, if Dookie threatened his position as cock of the walk.

The most innocent comment from Shahla would send me over the top like the time she saw me trying to give Dookie a bath. Dookie took off flying over our swimming pool so fast that I could not even see his feet. Shahla laughed and asked, "Do you think Dookie is a dog?"

I flew at her. "Don't you ever call Dookie a dog again!" I screamed as she took refuge behind Grandmother's skirts.

The only time I grudgingly allowed Shahla to touch Dookie was when I was playing with my other friend the football. Shahla would stroke him gently, but I snapped at her not to touch his tail feathers and scare him. I demanded to know if the water she brought him was "good water." I was too young to recognize that my behavior was a carbon copy of my hated father's when he was away from the house.

I thought of Dookie as another person and imagined that he suffered from the desert summer heat the same way I did, so when the coast was clear I would take him with me into the house to cool down, an act that my father had strictly forbidden. No strutting cock was going to invade his territory. Of course, telling me not to do something was tantamount to waving a red cape in front of a bull—until I was caught in the act of defiance.

"Get that thing out of this house!" Father shouted when he came home unexpectedly and caught Dookie and me inside. Then he narrowed his eyes into menacing slits and said, "If I catch that rooster in the house again, I will chop off his head." He had been drinking, of course, but there was a tone in his inebriated voice that made me scoop up Dookie and scurry outside, away from his demented threats.

War had been declared as far as I was concerned. My fear that Father would carry out his threat against Dookie lay like raw abrasives just under my skin. I knew beyond any shadow of a doubt that he was perfectly capable of killing anything I loved, and it would not take much to set him off in his constant state of inebriation. I recall asking my mother, my Grandmother, and even Shahla if they thought Father might kill Dookie and eat him, but the reassurances I got were far from comforting. I detected a note of apprehension in their voices and an attitude of brushing off the fears of a small boy. And I was small. It was David against my six-foot-one Goliath of a father that dared him to do anything to my beloved Dookie.

My abiding image of Father was a hulk of a man sprawled in his leather chair beside a small table holding up a half empty bottle of expensive imported whisky. Awake, his eyes were red and unfocused and he had trouble standing up; asleep, his mouth was parted emitting disgusting snores. I would look at that bottle he always kept just out of my reach as though he thought a small boy would be interested in drinking his precious liquid. What I actually wanted was to pour the contents down a drain and smash the bottle into millions of tiny pieces. In a very real way that bottle symbolized all I detested in the man from whose loins I had sprung.

Once I got the opportunity to express my opinion about the river of alcohol my father consumed daily. I discovered that he had been in the house and forgot to put his whisky bottle away when he left. Deliberately—was it gleefully?—I took the bottle, emptied its alcoholic contents down the drain and peed in the bottle, leaving an amber colored liquid the same shade as what I had poured out! I ran to tell Mother what I had done, and she only looked at me in horror. The next morning they took her to the clinic and she wore a bandage on her arm for six weeks thereafter.

I never learned the story of how my mother, twenty-eight years younger than my father, came to be married in a union I viewed as the perfect example of Beauty and the Beast. My resentment toward her came from her parental neglect rather than the physical and mental abuse I received from Father. The truth is that I hated them both and would gladly have run away given the opportunity, but my love for Grandmother and attachment to my beautiful, green-eyed sister immobilized me from that prospect. And, of course, there was Dookie who was probably much safer behind our compound walls than he would have been out on the streets.

"Grandmother," I asked one day, "Will Dookie die? Will you eat him if he dies?" Grandmother told me to put my hands together, which I did, and she took a pitcher of water and poured it over my hands letting me watch it slip through my fingers and fall to the floor. In her gentle voice, Grandmother said, "Life is water through your fingers. You follow its path. You choose its path as I poured water between your fingers. Yes. Dookie will die one day. Your mommy will die one day too. We are all mortals. No, we are not going to eat Dookie."

I mulled her words of wisdom over while feeling a pang of dread at the prospect of the eventual death of my beloved rooster but unconcerned about my mommy's death or mine, either, for that matter.

Summer was approaching that day when I came in from school and immediately started looking for my rooster friend. He was nowhere to be found and Grandmother gave me her usual answer, "Oh, he's around here somewhere." Father was at home and the servants were tiptoeing anxiously about the place from fear that they might wake him out of his drunken slumber.

I went back outside and renewed my search for Dookie. "Where are you, coward?" I called, "Where are you hiding? You've never done anything like this before. Are you angry because I went to school and left you alone?"

Dookie didn't answer. There was no movement in the garden. I was beginning to think Dookie had escaped over the walls and might be lost somewhere on the outside. I went back to the large storage building where Father kept some gardening tools when I saw some blood on the ground and smiled, thinking Father had cut himself. Still I could not locate my friend.

Bravely I went inside and marched into Father's presence where he sat drinking directly from his whisky bottle. "Where's Dookie?" I demanded. He grinned at me and answered, "There. On the table."

It was a large piece of fried chicken on a plate that he casually picked up and bit off a chunk of flesh. My eyes pooled with tears of rage. "You murdered my best friend!" I screamed, running at him like a Tasmanian devil, "You can't hurt me!" I kicked him hard in the shins, so hard that he slid out of his chair, kneeling on the floor which presented a second target that I kicked with deadly accuracy. Stupefied, Father clutched his groin and stared at me, unbelieving. It was the first time he had actually seen my rage that flame of hate I had kept buried inside me. I kicked him again and again until he was in so much pain he could not retaliate. Even his face was bloodied from my potent kicks. I didn't care. I wanted him dead! It took three of the servants to pull me away from my father's battered body.

There was no longer any reason for me to remain in that palatial prison. I ran miles from my house finally stopping under a small bridge where I fell into an exhausted sleep.

"Who is your father?" a voice came to me through my clouded head. Opening my eyes I looked up at a policeman. It was a typical question in this male dominant society I lived in. Who is your father? Translated, who owns you? I just stared up at him.

"Where is your house?" he demanded. Probably from the cut and obvious cost of my clothes, he recognized that I was no common street urchin. "What is that in your hand?" he asked, his voice getting gruffer as I just stared and refused to answer. I hated him, too, but he was a policeman; I was disoriented; and I knew I'd soon need something to eat. The policeman finally got enough information out of me that he took me none too gently back to my prison he called a home.

CHAPTER FOUR

FAMILY PLOTS

I WAS WEEKS IN ISOLATION EXCEPT FOR MY Grandmother who cared for me around the clock, but all her kindness and nurturing had little effect. I was anxious and mentally unstable, snapping at everything I came in contact with. I had a fixation on the kitchen knives and managed to conceal one long enough to confront my boozing father in his drinking place. It had been weeks since he last saw me, and if he thought my rage had subsided, he was in for a shock.

"I'll kill you!" I screamed at him, brandishing the knife, "I'll kill you the way you killed Dookie." Between the knife and the unadulterated hate radiating from my eyes, Father stood motionless, deathly afraid of coming near me. Grandmother had heard the commotion and managed to coax me out of the room. The booze and the Middle Eastern culture were, for once, working in my favor. Father had learned long ago that he could not hurt me when he staggered near and whapped me with his hand. It had gotten to the point where he could hardly stand up after delivering one of those ineffective blows. And in that culture, any man who murdered his own son would be an outcast; neither could he publically admit to being afraid of a young boy.

Afraid he was, however, a fact that kept him away from the house more than usual; and when he did come home, he had his alcohol moved to his room where he kept himself locked in, away from me. Of course all that pent up anger had to have an outlet, and my mother was the target of choice. His behavior toward her only served to deepen the contempt in which I held him.

Unable to get near him under the watchful eye of Grandmother—how could a blind woman see so much?—I nevertheless continued to plot my revenge. Grandmother, with her extrasensory perception, made it her task to keep me as far away from my father as possible for two people living in the same house, and she most certainly did not trust me around the kitchen knives.

In addition to the longer periods of Father's absence from the house, other things were changing as well. My martial arts classes had been cancelled, for one thing. Father had felt the strength of my kicks and no doubt dreaded helping me perfect that potent weapon. In place of the martial arts training, a dance instructor began coming to the house to teach Shahla and me the proper dance maneuvers. I did not object for I was aware that dancing in no way weakened the power of my legs.

Shahla, my dancing partner, became my new best friend. The beautiful green-eyed girl I had hurt so many times with my cold, harsh words was now my sounding board. The irony is that she got the position by default after the tragic murder of Dookie. It was amazing how she could love so deeply the little monster I had become, how she could be so gentle like Grandmother in the face of my often violent outbursts. I suppose we took well to dancing because she was so graceful in her movements and I was so athletic.

Grandmother loved to come into the room while the dance instructor was there. It amazes me to this day how a blind woman could watch us as we danced and even on occasion jump up to dance with us. I remember the lovely scent of her as she moved in time to the music like a kind of aroma therapy for my troubled soul. The dance instructions were an escape from the realities of our dysfunctional family, so Shahla and I entered into the practice with a willingness that bordered on pleasure.

I still had my other friend, the football that provided another kind of escape for me, though it was not nearly so placating. Kicking the ball, bouncing it on my knees, head, and chest, was far more aggressive than the gracefulness of the dance. When I kicked the football especially hard and watched it tumble down the little hill, was it my father's head I saw? I cannot answer that question. Most often, playing with the football was simply another escape for me, a time when I could be alone with this lifelong friend of mine, thinking of nothing but improving my control over the movements of the ball, feeling the strength growing in my agile legs and feet. Of course, I was not really alone during those times as Shahla was always there to watch me, sitting for hours by herself on the sidelines. How bored she must have been, but she never complained; and how little did I recognize or appreciate the depth of her love for me.

As fall approached, tensions grew stronger within the household. My drunken father was still so terrified of me that he seldom came home alone, usually accompanied by his brother. Both of them looked at me with suspicion, waiting, I suppose, for the other shoe to drop. Grandmother kept close tabs on me, keeping me as far away from Father and his brother as she could. That uncle, who had hardly ever visited us before, became almost a permanent resident in our house, further adding to the stress the family was already under. When Grandmother learned that my uncle had a mistress, she was not quiet in her condemnation and contempt, not only for him but also for my womanizing father. Grandmother, who had inherited a fortune from my late Grandfather, was one of the few women in our culture and society who had a certain amount of power because the circumstance gave her a modicum of independence, no longer the chattel property of a male.

Nevertheless, Grandmother was powerless to prevent Father's brother from coming into the house and whispering among themselves, looking at me with suspicion and diabolic intentions. Something was up, but we were not told anything about the content of the murmured plot that was taking shape.

PART II

EXILE

CHAPTER FIVE

STRANGER IN A STRANGE LAND

HATE AND FEAR ARE EACH STRONG EMOTIONS; PUT THEM together in one house and the air is charged with tension. I was nearing my seventh birthday and nothing had lessened my hatred for the murderer of my best friend, Dookie, nor Father's palpable fear of being alone in my presence. Odd that a small boy could cause such dread that Father's brother was constantly in the house, looking at me though slitted eyelids, and whispering guarded conversations that no one was supposed to hear. Whether she sensed it or actually overheard those conversations, Grandmother became visibly distressed, and, therefore, I knew something was up.

Grandmother seemed to hold onto me more than usual and Mother became more distant than ever. If Shahla knew what was being said, she never mentioned any of it to me. In a way I guess it was fortunate for me to be so consumed by my rage that most of what was going on escaped my notice—that is until the other shoe dropped. It was a scheme hatched up by Father's brother but left up to Grandmother to explain to me.

"Landy? What's Landy?" I asked.

"Not Landy, dear, London. London, England. Your father is planning to send you there to attend school. It's thousands of miles from here, Michael," Grandmother said, clutching my shoulders and barely able to keep a quiver out of her voice. I did not realize at the time, but in one fell swoop Father was getting his revenge on both me and Grandmother by almost literally tearing me out of her loving arms. Looking back, I suspect that Grandmother had a premonition that she would never run her fingers through my hair again.

As for me, the idea of being thousands of miles away from Dookie's murderer was almost as good as killing him with the same knife he used on my pet rooster. At age seven I was as hardened as an old man who had been through a war, nothing Father and his brothers could concoct could possibly bring fear into my heart. I did learn that Shahla was going with me, though I could not imagine why. She had never changed and still spoke softly and respectfully to Father. Was she just another thing in the way of his boozing and womanizing, a thorn that somehow pricked his black heart? I'll never know the answer to that question.

We were at the airport and Grandmother's hands had to be pried away from me, and I saw the tears forming in her sightless eyes. Mother was not there and Grandmother did not answer the questions I had about her. She only cried and held Shahla and me up to that last moment when we had to board the plane. I may not have known the meaning of the word, but instinctively I knew I was being sent into exile. And Shahla was banished as well because of me. Otherwise, no one would have even thought to drive her away with her sweet, uncomplaining nature.

There was nothing cheerful about London. To me it was ugly and dismal. We were met at the airport by an attractive brunette with a winning smile (who would become our governess, mother, and mentor) as we traveled to a small flat a block away from Hyde Park that was to be our home. Her name was Cilla and she did everything she could to help me settle in, but it was my guardian angel who helped me the most, my lovely sister, Shahla.

Cilla drove us to school, a huge campus for students K though 12 with the elementary section separated from the higher grades by a soccer field and a beautiful sports complex. I was in a foul mood already because I did not want to wear the required blue uniform with a white tie that I thought looked stupid and had cried tears to get out of wearing. I walked into that school building with an attitude of total disregard for anything or anyone. After all, I reasoned, this was definitely not a school of my choice. Ushered into my classroom, I came face to face with Mrs. Foresstes, a teacher of unlimited kindness and patience who had already been briefed that I was going to be a difficult student.

"Class, this is Mickey. Mickey La Vasani," she announced to the class.

"I'm not Mickey, I'm Michael La Vasani," I barked at her. She stood corrected and smiled benevolently at me in spite of my outburst.

The other students were about to learn of my nature as well when Mrs. Foresstes allowed me to choose my seat, one I found in the corner. Not only did I choose my place, I immediately set about seeing that I approved of those sitting near me, banishing several to other parts of the room. Cyclone Michael had arrived.

Mrs. Foresstes was an older lady with big glasses perched on her nose. I was amused by the fact that when she talked to the class, her chin almost rested on her chest. I soon came to realize that she was an especially kind person who loved her students, no matter how devious or troublesome they might be. Perhaps that is why I had been placed in her classroom. She never raised her voice which sometimes

27

made it difficult to understand what she was saying in her thick Scottish accent. But the thing about her that struck me the most was her patience with her students no matter how they behaved.

One of Mrs. Foresstes' habits was to write about her class in a journal every day. Some of the entries were quite amusing and I liked it when she wrote something about me—so much so that I endeavored to be the first student mentioned in her journal every day. Of course she always had something to say about me, for no matter how I liked Mrs. Foresstes, I was not about to turn into a docile lamb. Interestingly, she always managed to retain her sense of humor regardless of how frustrated she may have become at trying to deal with Michael La Vasani.

Well, like it or not, there I was in a school where the students were all different from me and all of us wearing stupid uniforms and shoes that we had to polish daily. We queued up for everything, marching here and there like the daily trip to chapel to pray and the procession to the dining room for lunch. It was not long before I zeroed in on the enemy—the principal of the school—and I became his living nightmare. The surest way to get me to do something was to tell me not to do it. I broke all the rules as the number one trouble maker in a perfectly proper British school. How different I was from that angel, that model of perfect behavior, my sister Shahla. Yet it did not escape my notice that no matter what I did, the British stiff upper lip always seemed to handle it. I suspected that Father had donated a vast sum of money to the school which was covering a multitude of my sins. Nevertheless, I had a very difficult time of adjusting and Shahla was constantly being called into the principal's office to help me out of my most recent peccadillo.

By the time mid winter rolled around, it was very cold in London, though neither Shahla nor I minded the weather all that much.

Although it was some distance to the school, we always walked, taking the long way around so we could pass by the River Thames. It wasn't just the Thames, however, that drew us there, it was also a small kiosk where we could buy the most delicious hot turkey sandwiches, which we both adored. Not only that, the man who ran the kiosk was a large, dark complexioned Indian man named Roj who was always jolly and happy to see us. How different he was from the Fat Man back home. As we walked away from his kiosk every morning, Roj would call out our names until one morning we turned to see what he wanted. Flashing his gleaming smile at us, he blew us a friendly kiss. Shahla and I always liked Roj.

Nevertheless, the ember still burned in my gut, my rage was just beneath the surface and could erupt at any moment, out of control and threatening both to me and anyone around me. Had it not been for Shahla, I have no idea what might have become of me. Alone in a boarding school, with no one who cared for me enough to calm my violent heart, there is no telling how different my life story might have played out. It was bad enough as it was. I walked into my classroom one morning and there was a pretty little girl sitting in my chair, the one I had selected and dictated who could sit next to me. As I marched to where she was sitting, my face must have held a terrifying expression because her eyes widened with fear. I didn't care. It made no difference to me that she was a girl or that she was very pretty on top of that. She was occupying my space, and there was no way I was going to let this breech go uncorrected.

"You're sitting in my chair," I stormed at the girl, paying no attention to Mrs. Foresstes who tried to mollify the situation in her calm, sweet voice. The girl jumped up and took a seat next to the window that looked out onto the school yard. Regardless, I ended up back in the principal's office who looked at me with consternation, no longer sure of what to do with me. In the fuss over the chair, I did find out that the pretty girl's name was Hailie and that she was just a month older than me. We were later to become friends.

On the way home after school that day, Shahla pleaded with me, "Michael, please, please, don't cause any more trouble." I protested my innocence, but she became more eloquent and convincing in her arguments against my unruly behavior. I felt as though a proud God were screaming at the man, pointing out that there was an angel walking along in the form of an innocent girl and I was walking with her, the creation God was so proud of. That was the way I had come to view Shahla, as a wingless angel whose spirit soared above the clouds with the very soul of the Virgin in her beatific, beautiful face.

We were taking the long way back to our flat along the Thames and found a bench where we sat for a while watching the flowing water and talking about Dookie and Grandmother. The conversation and the nearness of Shahla calmed the beast within my soul, and I could remember the pleasures of touching Dookie's brilliant feathers and the warm feeling of Grandmother's fingers running through my hair. However, in spite of the light Shahla brought into my life, the storm clouds were always just over the horizon.

My next episode involved the other great love of my life—football. Every day I passed by the playing field and saw the boys enjoying the game, and I wanted to be out there with them, using the natural talent I had for the game. I asked Mrs. Foresstes to get me placed on the team, but the coach objected because of my age. He would not even consent to a tryout for me, and the ember began to glow. Every day I saw the boys playing soccer and every day my rage grew a little bit more at those who were thwarting my intense desire to join in the games. I finally snapped one afternoon after school. A game was going on at the soccer field and I just marched right onto it, mindless of the fact that I was disrupting the game in progress.

"Hey, you! Get off the field! Can't you see a game is going on?" It was the referee, but I ignored him and kept walking. When I got face to face with him, he was standing, glaring down at me. In a flash, however, he was on the ground, the surrogate father I wanted to crush, as my strong legs lashed out, hurting him any way I could—again, and again, and again. They carried him off the field on a stretcher. So there I was back on the principal's hands, an ill behaved monster he had no idea how to deal with.

"Why didn't you just ask to play on the team?" he demanded.

"I did! They wouldn't even let me try out!" I snapped back.

Out of desperation, I suppose, and after much wrangling with the coach, I was allowed to play with the team, and they discovered that I was a natural player—fast and furious—connected to the ball from hours and hours of practice. Although I was the youngest player on the team, I soon became the captain simply because I was the best. The coach was in a quandary seeing his team win games yet wanting to get rid of me for defying him in the first place. I was a constant reminder that a small boy had gone over his head to have a place on his team, and for all his bluster and posturing, I suspect he was also a little afraid of me as well.

They say that abused children will gladly return to their abusive homes because that is their reality, all they know about life and living. If I wanted to return to the abuse, it would only have been to give me an opportunity to avenge the death of Dookie. Nevertheless, in spite of the football, I was homesick which actually increased with Grandmother's frequent telephone calls.

"How are you, Grandmother? I miss you. Why don't you come here and stay with me and Shahla? Cilla can't cook, Grandmother.

I'm hungry for your food." The conversations went the same way every time she called, and her answers were always the same, "Be a good boy, Michael. You're a man now and you must watch out for your sister." And, of course I listened, but I missed her blue eyes. In spite of missing Grandmother so much and never acquiring a taste for Cilla's cooking, my life went on.

CHAPTER SIX

CRASH AND BURN

I ENTERED A PERIOD OF MY LIFE WHEN THE EMBER cooled a bit and I was relatively happy. It began one afternoon when Shahla introduced me to a new friend.

"Michael, this is Hailie McCartney," she said, presenting the same lovely little girl I had terrorized in my classroom, "She's a neighbor of ours. Isn't she in your classroom at school?" This time I really looked at her, a perfect little Barbie doll of a girl who smiled at me as though the chair incident had never happened. From that day on, it was even more fun to sit on our bench by the Thames and watch the boats drift by as I perched there between two beautiful angels who made me laugh instead of rage. We laughed a lot and I learned that Hailie's parents were both doctors, very hospitable people who welcomed Shahla and me into their home. It was my chance to see that not all families are dysfunctional war zones, that love is possible between a family of people who live together in the same house and consider each other's feelings. It was such a warm, friendly environment, and my sister and I became almost like members of their family. Hailie and I laughed long and loud so much that her parents accused us of being heard for blocks away. I loved to tease Hailie.

"I baked you some cookies!" she said proudly one day.

"Huh! Your mother baked them and you are taking the credit," I retorted.

Hailie only laughed at my teasing, though, and our friendship grew by the day. It was also gratifying to me to see Shahla looking so happy. It was as though the McCartney household had become a kind of sanctuary for us both, two children who had never suspected that family life could be so comforting and so much fun.

One evening after a soccer game, the school bus dropped me off in front or our flat and I was surprised to see it all dark inside. I opened the door cautiously, fearing that something was wrong, when suddenly the lights went on and people jumped up and yelled, "Surprise!" It was a party organized just for me! The McCartneys had planned the whole thing, something that I had never experienced in my life before, and I was literally stunned. Shahla came and hugged me, calling me "the soccer champion" and everyone was congratulating me in the most pleasant ways. Hailie brought me a beautifully wrapped box that was large but not very heavy. I stood there just staring down at the box, but Hailie urged me by saying, "Open it! It's something for you!"

When I got it opened, I was unable to speak, for there in the box was a beautiful golden colored football like I had never seen in my life. I didn't even know that soccer balls came in such a color. Hailie knew that I would appreciate this gift more than any other thing she might have chosen to give me, and she was so right. That ball became my constant companion—I even slept with it and carried it to school with me every day. Life was changing for me in positive ways that I did not recognize, though I never stopped causing trouble at school even though my marks were so high the teachers were calling me "Super Kid," or that my soccer team was constantly winning games. The mischief bred in me from my early upbringing simply would not go away and the principal dubbed me the "Oh, no, Kid." That, I guess, was because when he saw me coming, he would think, "Oh, no, what has Michael done this time." To tell the truth, though, I was thoroughly enjoying my time with Shahla and Hailie and all the attention I was getting at school. I was the football hero, the gifted child who could solve difficult math problems, and the lucky boy always seen in the company of two very beautiful girls. My nerves were quieting, I was gaining more control of myself, but disaster was just around the corner.

I was playing in a school football tournament and we were winning when suddenly I was called out of the game. "Subbed out!" I thought angrily, "Nobody subs me! I'm the captain, the Super Kid! They can't do this to me!" I was furious and yelling at the coach who calmly told me that Shahla had taken ill at school and I was to be taken to her at the hospital. "Shahla? In the hospital?" I was scared and confused. I didn't like hospitals, the smell, the memories of going with Mother to have her arm sewed up, the Fat Man in the clinic. No, hospitals were not places where I wanted to be. All the way to the dreaded place I tried to imagine what had happened to my beloved sister, hoping for the best but fearing the worst.

When I walked into her room, I saw her looking pale and very, very sick. Hailie was there in the room with her and she spoke quickly, "Michael, she'll be fine. My Dad is here." And Shahla tried to smile at me through her pain that I did not dare ask her about. I sat down beside her bed and held her hand, thinking how Shahla was a mirror image of me, tough and a fighter, a survivor of our terrible childhoods. She showed no pain and held back the tears because that was the way we were, conditioned to difficulties and hurt.

35

After a few days, Shahla was released from the hospital and I imagined that life was back to normal, never asking questions for fear of hearing the answers. The three of us—Shahla, Hailie, and me—were back together, sitting on the bench by the Thames, eating Roj's hot turkey sandwiches, and laughing.

One day, Shahla and I were walking back home along the banks of the Thames when she spotted an impoverished woman and her little daughter sitting on the pavement, begging for money. I was aghast that Shahla walked over toward them.

"No!" I shouted, "I don't want to talk to them! Let's go home!" But Shahla walked on as though she never heard my protests.

She talked to the little girl, "How old are you?"

"Ten," answered the shivering child. It was very cold that evening.

"Do you go to school?" Shahla asked.

The little girl said nothing, just sat there staring at her mother, unsure how to respond to Shahla's question. I watched with a mixture of awe and disgust as my beautiful sister removed her hat and coat and gave them to the girl. "Keep yourself warm, darling," she said.

"Are you crazy?" I shouted at Shahla.

She turned to me and asked, "Do you have any money?"

I took the change I had out of my pocket and gave it all to her, and she turned and handed the money to the pitiful woman. Then we walked on home in the freezing cold because now we had no money to take the bus. It would be years later before I began to understand the magnitude of my sister's love for all human beings.

It was the very strong bond between Shahla and me that allowed me to hand over my last bit of pocket money so she could give it to the beggar lady. I would no more have done that for anyone else (with the possible exception of Grandmother) than I would have gladly handed over my new gold colored football. Shahla had become my protector and mentor; I listened to her even if I did not always follow her advice. As much as I wanted to please her, the rage was too near the surface, and there were times when I just couldn't help myself from getting into trouble again. Nevertheless, I took great pride in Shahla, the princess of our school, the angel in the form of a beautiful young lady. When I walked home with Shahla and Hailie, I walked on air, knowing that other boys were green with envy and would have given anything to trade places with me. Shahla and Michael—the odd couple, the soft spoken, always polite girl with her raging demon of a brother she was always snatching from the fire. Whenever we were together, I was able to compromise my self-centered and angry behavior; it was when we were apart that I frequently lost control, wrecking havoc in every direction around me. Only Shahla and Grandmother ever saw the vulnerability in me; I made sure that everyone else felt a tinge of terror whenever they saw me coming.

The day my world began to unravel further began like any ordinary day. Shahla and I had come to school together, and I was sitting in my classroom being reasonably studious when the principal called me out of class.

"Your sister collapsed in class this morning and she's in hospital. Since you are her only relative in the country, I think it best that you go to be with her," he said as we climbed into his car for him to drive me personally to the dreaded hospital. Once at the hospital, the doctor, who I thought looked like a mouse with a large nose, tried to explain to me what was happening to Shahla.

"Are you telling me the truth?" I demanded, used to adults glossing things over for children in what they considered the thing to do.

"She will be fine, son," the doctor assured me.

"I'm not your son," I snapped, "Just do your job!"

37

Shahla, lying in the bed with all sorts of wires and tubes running from her to machines and IV bottles, was not pleased with my behavior, and I apologized, "I'm sorry, Sis. I just don't know any better." I felt so helpless, unsure how to accommodate Shahla looking so pale and listless, though in good spirits, which I suspect were for my benefit. I actually felt her pain and I finally fell asleep there beside her, drifting off with the thought in my brain that the love of my life was terribly ill and I was helpless to do anything for her.

This time Hailie did not come to the hospital. Was it because her parents knew something about the seriousness of Shahla's condition and thought it would be too much for her to deal with me, sidestepping my questions? Perhaps it was my usual behavior that they did not want Hailie exposed to as I shouted orders at the hospital staff simply because I had never been taught how to ask for anything. I had been raised as the little lord of the household, ordering the servants around whenever I wanted the least thing. Now here I was an eight-year-old little monster with the mind of an adult trapped in an impossible situation I had no idea how to deal with.

I dreamed in my sleep. I was playing soccer in the snow. I was dreadfully cold and I tried to run so I could warm up. But something was holding me. I could not run. I was trapped by something or someone holding me, but I could not see who or what it was. I was breathing hard when I heard a voice calling me through the dark veil of my dream.

"Michael! Michael! I'm okay. You go on home, now."

It was Shahla bringing me back from my terrible nightmare. "We'll go home together tomorrow," I said solemnly.

Then out of the blue, Hailie showed up with her arm in a cast, explaining why she had not come sooner. She never told me, but much later I learned that she had fallen on the stairs rushing to bring cookies to me at the hospital.

As far as I knew after that brief stay in the hospital, our lives were all back to normal. We settled into the same routine I had become accustomed to in London—Shahla and I doing our lessons after school, and Shahla screaming at the top of her lungs during my football games whenever I scored a goal. Hailie was always there, too, with her arms waving above her pretty head as the crowd cheered us on. Much later I learned that Shahla actually never enjoyed football, she only attended games to support me.

The English Schools Tournament was coming up in Manchester and I was all excited about going with my team when Shahla informed me that she would not be going along this time. "Hailie will be there and you can tell me all about it when you return. You go and have a good time . . . and win!" Shahla said. She grabbed me and hugged me for a long time before letting me go, and I thought something was strange, but my mind was centered on the tournament. I will never forget those few seconds with Shahla holding me close that day.

It was a record hot summer in England during that time which may have bothered some of the other players in the tournament, but certainly not me. Over the course of eleven days, our school handily won the tournament and the announcers made a great deal out of my being the youngest and best player in the tournament. Some of them even suggested that I could have won the tournament all by myself, a comment I made sure all the other boys on my team knew about.

If life were a movie, what happened as I ran into the flat to tell Shahla about the soccer tournament would be played in slow motion. The apartment was still as death and the Beast was sitting in our parlor. I had not spoken a word to him since Shahla and I had been packed off to London and I was not about to start now.

"Shahla!" I called. There was no answer. "Where is Shahla?" I asked of the walls, not looking at Dookie's murderer.

I vaguely heard his voice coming through the echo chamber of my mind, "She's not here."

"Cilla!" I called, "where are you?"

There was no answer. I was alone in the apartment with the one person in the world I hated the most. I ran to Shahla's room and slept there that night, confused, miserable, for I could get no information as to Shahla's whereabouts. It was a long, terrible night of tossing and turning until, exhausted, I finally drifted off to sleep.

"Hey, Mr. Bear, are you done hibernating? We're late for school!" Hailie's voice came through the mist that shrouded my mind. Hailie, as usual, was smiling at me as I looked for something to eat, but Cilla was not in the flat. I was hungry, anxious, disturbed, and confused, and no one was there to give me any answers. Somehow I made it through the school day, determined to get those answers when I returned to the flat that evening.

Cilla was there when I got home, but no amount of bullying on my part could get a word out of her about Shahla. Everywhere there was a wall of impenetrable silence built around this eight-year-old boy. Even though I stayed at Hailie's house, there was no information coming from her doctor parents. Nobody could or would tell me anything about Shahla. I was a consummate ball of misery, made even more miserable by the unexpected visit from Mrs. Foresstes, who had never paid a home visit to me before. It did not help that everyone tried to keep me occupied with my mind off of Shahla and her whereabouts which only added to my confusion and anger.

Then one afternoon as I closed the door to our apartment I nearly jumped out of my skin when I heard a familiar voice behind me, "Hey, you handsome champion!"

I turned around to see Shahla sitting in a wheelchair being pushed by Father with a nurse in tow, carrying a large bag. I rushed to embrace my beautiful sister and vaguely heard Father say, "Be careful with her."

I stepped back and looked at her. She was heavily wrapped in bandages, not like the ones I always had on when I played football.

"You look like an Egyptian mummy!" I said.

My comment amused Shahla and she smiled, but then she said, "I'm going to bed, Michael."

"Hey, we're the champions! Do you want to see the trophy?" I was bubbling over with all the things I had wanted to share with her all the time she had gone missing.

"Later," she smiled, and was taken to her room. I wanted to stay with her, but Father was there and I could not bear being in the same room with him.

Shahla did not go to school for two weeks, and because Father was camped out at our place, I rarely got to see her. He did not drink at the flat, but I could smell it on his breath and would have kicked him again had it not been for my sick sister. Life was almost intolerable during that time. I kept myself locked away in my room to avoid contact with my father, aching to spend time with my beloved sister.

Then one morning I heard Shahla calling me, "Come on, Michael, we're going to be late for school."

I bolted out of my room and came face to face with her standing in the hallway, dressed in her school uniform. But something confused me. At first I thought I was dreaming; then I imagined she was playing some sort of joke on me. What I saw was the scariest thing I had ever seen in my life and I did not want to touch her.

"Where's your arm?" I stammered. I thought I would wet my pants seeing her there with one sleeve of her school uniform blouse draping empty where her arm should have been. I still thought it was some kind of dirty joke she was playing on me. "How do you do that?"

"Michael," Shahla said softly, "they had to cut off my arm. I had cancer. It was in my arm and they gave me the choice of removing the arm or having it spread to my whole body. It was a simple choice for me to lose the arm under those circumstances."

Father stood there smiling as she gave me the information everyone had shielded me from up to that moment.

I had suffered pain from Father's abuse and from playing in tough football games, and I had never let anyone see my hurt or the tears I cried alone in my room at night. But nothing in my life prepared me for the pain I felt at that moment seeing my beautiful sister standing there, mutilated and brave. There was no way I could hide the tears that began to flow at that moment. Even the rage could not dislodge me from the spot where I was frozen to the floor, hearing Shahla's gentle voice, and aware of Father's evil smile as he enjoyed seeing me in mental anguish, knowing I was hurting far more than anything he had ever been able to inflict with the back of his hand. For many years to come my sweet dreams of playing on the soccer pitch evolved into nightmares of seeing myself skewered on a rotisserie slowly roasting as I spun around and around.

Hailie became my refuge, my substitute angel, and some of my enthusiasm returned when a trip to her family's country place in Wales during school holidays entered the planning stages. We tried to interest Shahla into going along with us, talking excitedly about all the things we could do in the country, but Shahla adamantly refused to consider it. When I realized that our excitement and urging were making her uncomfortable, I backed off, thinking I would go when school was out for the holidays and tell Shahla all about our adventures.

Shahla never tried to hide her prosthetic arm, but she became more and more reclusive, no longer attending my football games and often missing days at a time from school. Her teachers were like butterflies around her, coming to the flat and helping her with her school work. When she was able to attend class, our walks along the Thames to our flat became slower and slower, and she seemed to age. One day leaving school, Shahla suggested we take the double-decker home and we never walked along the Thames again.

As soccer was to me, so writing was to Shahla. She put everything down in poetic form in both her poetry and her articles in the monthly journals of our school. Her pen name was S. Lahore in tribute to her favorite author, Jena Lahore, and students and teachers alike would wait anxiously to see what she wrote next. It was difficult for her after her writing arm was amputated, but she persisted, refusing my offers to help her. She took writing classes to improve her style, and in spite of her handicap continued to pen her inspirational messages, an avocation that brought the only light left in her debilitating life.

It was time for the trip to Wales and my excitement level ran high. Maybe by the time I returned, the Beast would be out of our flat and back where he belonged. Shahla seemed happy to remain behind and catch up on the school work she had missed because of her illness. For ten glorious days at the country estate in Wales, Hailie and I went riding and playing around in the beautiful grounds. Even though I missed Shahla, Hailie did her best to fill my days with plenty of things to do. I even got to play football in a local game.

Red carded! The Welsh referee seemed gleeful to kick me out of the game. "Is the man blind?" I asked Hailie, "I only gave that boy a gentle push!"

"You call that a gently push?" she asked, smiling, "They carried him out on a stretcher." My jersey was as muddy as my mood that day.

Summertime in Wales brought another experience into my life as Hailie and I sat together outside on the cool, damp grass. I worried about Hailie. "You're going to be cold," I said.

"Then hold my hand," she replied.

I took her hand in mine and looked into her beautiful face, "I like it here in Wales. And I like you."

It was slow motion time again as I leaned toward her and gave her a kiss, the first time I had kissed a girl who was not my relative. That magical time in a boy's life when, later, he imagines the whole thing was a dream. But it was not a dream as I felt her delicate, little fingers running through my curly hair.

The drive back from Wales to London was excruciatingly long when no amount of distraction could erase the anxiety of seeing Shahla and knowing how she was getting along. I wanted to be in her room, telling her about the estate, the horseback riding, the stupid referee who gave me a red card, and maybe even about the kiss. I was never good at telling her how much I loved her, but I felt sure she would understand as I shared my life of the last ten days with her.

Finally arriving back in front of our flat, I barged in the house calling her name. No answer. Cilla was not there either. There was nothing for me to do but confront the drunken monster sitting in the semi-darkness.

"Where is she?" I demanded of Father, "Where's Shahla?"

"She's not here," he slurred.

I ran to her room to see for myself and ran back, demanding an explanation for her absence. What was I feeling? Was I ready to walk the long distance to the hospital where she likely was? Or was some other dread building up in me, a nameless fear that clutched my chest like a cold, hard vice?

"Tell me where she is!" I shouted at Father.

"She's gone," he replied.

"Gone? Gone where?"

"Gone for good. She's dead," he said with a grim glee, watching to see how the news would shatter me, hoping to see me finally break down in his presence.

What he saw, however, was another eruption of my unmitigated rage. I flew at him kicking and swinging, intent on destroying him once and for all. "You're a bloody, drunken liar!" I screamed. I kicked him so hard even I could feel his pain. I grabbed his hair and pulled as I bit him as hard as I could. I wanted him dead, as dead as his own cold, harsh words. Out of self protection he threw me off violently, so much so that I hit my head on something solid and passed out.

When I awoke, Cilla was sitting beside my bed holding my hand. "He's lying to me, Cilla? Why? Where's Shahla?" Cilla held my hand tighter but said nothing. How could a rational person deal with the cruelty of my dysfunctional family? How could she explain a father so vengeful that he actually enjoyed seeing his eight-year-old son's misery? How could she tell the boy that he would never see his sister again, that her body had been flown back to the Middle East for burial?

The exile was now complete. I was finally alone. I was a vegetable he chewed harder to make me feel the pain.

As a player, I never knew the word, surrender. With me it was play to win and play to the bitter end. What I was up against now in a mingling of hate and rage turned out to be bigger than my will to win, probably out of the frustration of the inability to inflict any more pain on my mortal enemy, my father. The madness crept up on me as the hallucinations of my dreams punctuated by fearful screams became the vision of my waking hours as well. Everyone I saw began to look like Father, they spoke with his voice, and they all appeared drunk on strong drink. My behavior was erratic and schizophrenic, driven by a blinding desire to avenge my beautiful sister, my lost angel and friend. No one was really safe around me.

CHAPTER SEVEN

ON THE EDGE

I WENT BACK TO WALKING ALONG THE THAMES, BUT IT was no longer a peaceful walk as memories of Shahla flooded my very soul, and I cursed and screamed against the unfairness that had been dealt me like a death sentence. I became a wrecking machine, kicking and breaking everything fragile within my reach. I broke glass, perhaps because glass formed the container of his vile whisky, and I bit everyone who came close enough to my fearsome jaws. In my mind's eye, the people I bit were manifestations of him who had flown back to the Middle East and abandoned me to my hate and grief. I saw the poor little beggar girl wearing Shahla's hat and I charged her, trying to get back something that was hers. The police came and took me away, an eight-year-old prisoner without crimes he could be charged with.

The local constables feared me after the numerous times they were forced to answer the hysterical calls from school or neighbors who could not deter me from my violent behavior. All the constables had bite marks on their arms or remembered the pain of my kicks to their groins. I was the wild bird with clipped wings that had been mercilessly shoved from the only nest I ever knew, and I could only lash out in bitter frustration at my inability to destroy the beast that was destroying me.

Whatever contribution my father had made to my school was not enough to prevent my being expelled after I started a fire in the hundred-year-old school library that destroyed volumes of respected literature. That was the final straw that put me into a straight jacket to prevent me from harming others, and possibly myself. The hospitals tried valiantly to do something to calm my destructive soul, but all to no avail. I was not only a stranger in a strange city, I was a psychiatric enigma that no medical professional had a clue how to handle. I was kept in isolation with people guarding me who had all felt the pain of my wrath and had sustained the injuries to prove it. For two months, I remained in this limbo that did nothing to bring me down from the terrible heights of anguish and impotent rage. I can only imagine that the hospital administration in desperation notified my father that he would have to do something with me; that they could not keep me indefinitely since I was completely unresponsive to every treatment they tried.

Predictably, it was not my father who came to take me away from my hospital incarceration, it was Father's brother and best friend, my uncle that I detested almost as much as I did Father. My intelligence overruled my insanity when I realized my only chance of getting out of that place and not be put into another one just like it lay in my ability to control myself. If I was crazy, I certainly was not stupid.

My uncle did not talk to me. He swept in and gave orders to prepare me, not revealing what he was up to, which roused all sorts of suspicions in my mind and made it even harder to try to behave. On the way to the airport, I asked him where we were going to go, but he refused to answer. He was the deadly businessman and inveterate politician, a calculating monster with several layers of dragon-like skin. He was not a hallucination, he actually did look just like Father, and I hated him with slightly less venom than that I felt for his brother. I tapped him on the shoulder and consciously used the facial expression that everyone who knew me had learned to regard with a certain fear of what might happen.

"Where are we going?" I asked again.

"Hong Kong," he replied curtly.

Without a clue what or where Hong Kong was, I figured it had to be better than being in a straight jacket in some psychiatric ward, so I determined to bear with my uncle until I got the chance to hurt him, something I wanted desperately to do. The flight was terribly long and, sitting beside my uncle, I did not want to look at him and tried to sleep. Unfortunately, my sleep was tortured by visions of my father pulling me away from my armless sister. When we landed in Hong Kong, there was a car waiting for us that took us directly to a strange looking building with colorful tiles and statues of lions and dragons everywhere. The moment I had been handed over to some weird looking bald men dressed in odd clothes, my uncle rushed away. Although I was happy to see him leave, I thought about saying good-bye to him by introducing him to the steel toed foot of my right leg, but refrained from doing so. Later, I felt really bad that I had let that moment get away.

At the moment, though, I had other matters to consider like why I was here and who the strange looking people were and where were they taking me? Had I been sold as a slave to this bald-headed monkeys wrapped up in orange sheets? Why, when I tried to ask questions did they only put their hands together and bow? What kind of nonsense was that? What was this odd place where I had been dropped off like a bundle of London Times on a cold pavement? The colorful flags and paintings might otherwise have enthralled an eight-year-old heart, but at that moment they were frightening reminders that I had landed alone in a world as foreign to me as the dark side of the moon. There were hundreds of people milling about and weird looking bicycles everywhere, but there was no one to explain to me where I was or why I was there. My imagination ran away with me, leaving me more frightened than I had ever been in my life, though I was hardly about to show my distress to anyone. I was now in China, one of the most mysterious places on the planet for most westerners, and instinctively I knew that whatever was about to happen to me would pass unnoticed by anyone who had ever known me in my young life. Maybe Mrs. Foresstes might wonder about me in a fleeting moment as she received new students into her classroom. Perhaps my mother might think about asking my father where I was. Grandmother, if she was still alive, would be the only person whose thoughts were with me night and day, but I was sure she had no idea what had become of me. It did not take long for the realization to sink in on me that I was totally, dreadfully, and inescapably alone in the world.

That night, I slept in that strange and colorful building where an old Chinese woman watched over me and fed me strange food that I found to be palatable. The bald men in orange sheets watched me from afar as though they had been warned of my volatile temper. My gut reaction was that for now at least I needed to hang out with these monkey men who at least seemed to have some idea of who I was and that I needed supervision. The next morning, two of the robed men took me again to the airport where we boarded a plane that flew to a destination I was unable to identify. My imagination kicked in and I thought I had been sold to a Chinese mobster to be his personal boss boy, an idea that certainly had no appeal to a kid who had ordered other people around all his life.

On the ground, we traveled by Shank's Mare, first taking an interminably long ferry ride that landed at what looked to me like a fishing village that we hiked around and headed out into a deserted landscape. We walked for days and there were blisters on my feet, but I was mute and non-combative as I suffered the pain, refusing to complain or let the strange men know. My physical training, I was sure, made me stronger and better than those mysterious men who never seemed to tire as we continued walking, walking, walking. I kept reminding myself that I was the captain, the invincible, the boy that everyone feared . . . but why didn't these weird guys not seem afraid of me?

To distract myself, I started throwing stones at the golden monkeys we encountered along our route. They were unlike the cute little monkeys I had seen at the London Zoo. These were long and sinewy with reddish blond and very scraggy hair that made them look like something out of a horror film. Their faces were like those of the wizened old men I had seen in the souks of Iran, sitting around sucking on their hookahs muttering platitudes out of the Quran. Their shrieks were raucous howls that grated on my nerves. I threw stones with deadly accuracy, making them yell in protest and pain. The two men I was following turned and made disapproving faces at me, admonishing me in a language I did not understand.

There were millions of butterflies I tried to knock down with stones as well. When I could not throw stones for one reason or another, I made loud noises to scare the monkeys and butterflies away as though they were in my space rather than the other way around. The men in robes paid me no more mind and we continued walking, walking, and walking. The terrain was becoming more and more daunting with large rocks and boulders that punished my feet through the thick soles of my boots. The monkey men were almost barefooted and did not seem to mind the hard, stony path we cut through the landscape.

Late in the evenings, we stopped to make camp. It was hideously cold and I was freezing, but when the men in the flimsy robes showed no sign of being affected by the cold, I was determined to show them that I was far more rugged than they. It may sound like arrogance—and I'm sure there was a lot of that in me at the time—but in reality is was the last self-defense of an eight-year-old boy who had been banished to the back of beyond and totally dependent on these silent men who reminded me of the golden monkeys I had thrown stones at earlier. Except the monkeys in the distance were not silent, chattering in their ear piercing voices, communicating with one another. It seemed to me that the three of us were more like animals than the monkeys because no attempt at any verbal communication took place. I sat there shivering in the darkness, so black that it seemed to me that the light had taken the day off, closing everything up except the faint orange glow of the little fire the men had built. The one thing I refused to admit to myself was that I was scared right down to my bones.

Toward the end of our horrendous hike through what I was sure was some of the most rugged terrain on earth, we started climbing a hill drawing nearer and nearer to a sight that amazed me. It looked to me like a Hollywood movie set, but nothing like the fantastic beauty of a Shangri-La. Instead it was a massive citadel in the distance that appeared to be carved right out of the side of a sheer cliff, surrounded by incredibly high snow-capped mountains which I would later learn were the Himalayas. We were going up the only way possible to reach that castle of stone much larger than any I had ever seen in England. I noticed a second trail that continued upward from the other side of the grand structure, but only the most expert of mountain climbers could have arrived at that place if not for the narrow trail we followed. I imagined it was what the city of Troy must have looked like to Agamemnon, as he led his Achaeans on the quest to retrieve the beautiful Helen. The more we traveled toward that isolated place, the further off it seemed. When at long last we neared the entrance to this gargantuan structure, someone lowered a drawbridge that stretched over a ravine below lined with vicious spikes that would impale anyone who happened to fall from the bridge. Similar spikes protruded from the walls of that great fortress as well. No one would enter there unless the people inside allowed it. No, it was not Shangri-La or even a Hollywood romantic adventure—it was much more like Dante's Descent into Hell. Just as I had learned from my father and from playing soccer not to fear physical pain, I think as I passed over that drawbridge, I learned not to fear death.

If the place seemed to me like some kind of hell, I was about to become the Devil incarnate. As we entered the cavernous building, the drawbridge was raised behind us and the gates were closed. My thought at the moment was that this certainly was a different looking psychiatric center, and I fully expected to see a bedlam of mad men racing around and making hideous noises. That anticipation was as fruitless as my wistful thought of being Aladdin able to open the gates and let down the drawbridge by simply saying, "Open, Sesame." The place was deathly quiet, although there were dozens of those men and boys dressed in orange or brown robes milling around intent on various tasks. Unwanted, unloved, and uncared for created a hunger in me far more painful than not having food to eat, and to this day I cannot really articulate the great emptiness at that moment inside my boyish soul.

CHAPTER EIGHT

THE EVIL DEEDS

Not in the air, nor ocean-midst,
Nor hidden in the mountain clefts,
Nowhere is found a place on earth,
Where man is freed from evil deeds.
Buddha

"HELLO, MY NAME IS WBISO," SAID THE LITTLE MAN IN a brown robe and carrying a sturdy bamboo stick. "I'm the gong ringer," he said with a touch too much pride. I was to become quite familiar with that bamboo stick as he used it for more than just striking a gong. His accent was so thick I could hardly understand a word he said in the closest thing to English I had heard since leaving Hong Kong.

"You stay those boys," Wbiso went on, pointing to a group of boys across the great expanse of the fortress from which I could never go home or even open the gate. Boys dressed in brown robes, heads shaven—boys with stories behind how they came to be here—boys who did not speak my language—strange boys, not ones like the football players I was familiar with. That is what I saw and the red rage of anger boiled over in me. I was not going down without a fight!

Wbiso pulled at my hand to lead me over to those boys with whom I was supposed to live, and that was his mistake. I hit him so hard that all he could do was bend over and fall down on the dirt floor, my footprint marked his neck, and I shall never forget the look of agony and surprise on his pitiful face. I cared not in the least what he suffered or what I had done by way of announcing my arrival in either a psychiatric ward or an orphanage that I still was not sure which one it was. It did not register on me at the moment that this forsaken place that is not even on a map would be my home for many years to come.

I am the little spring that moves the ocean banks
I was the lava born of the ocean depths
I shall bring offerings of pain for I am the god of pain
I am a flightless bird landing where there is no land
I sing songs where no words are found

My bed was in the corner of that vast rectangular prison—that was the way I thought of it at the time—with blocked walls decorated by bamboo coverings. My bed was a rolled up thin cotton blanket with a hard tube shaped pillow, and it was cold because what little heat there was rose up to the top of what appeared to me to be thirty-foot walls with no ceiling. The Tower of London, which I had visited, was warmer than this place that I learned much later had been built centuries before by Mogul warriors as a guardhouse and observation platform which explained the sharp spikes and heavy drawbridge. As an observation platform, it was ideally suited to give a magnificent view of the valley below and, as I mentioned earlier, the only access from below was the narrow trail gorged out of the crags of the hill that still did not provide entrance unless the heavy drawbridge was lowered in welcome. Someone could, if there were anyone up there, come down the mountain by a trail that ended at the back of the forbidding fortress. Within those four uncovered walls the wind never stopped howling its pitiless lament, giving the place a surreal atmosphere of having gone back in time some centuries ago. It rained often, sharp stinging droplets like pellets of sleet, and on many days the fog was so thick inside those walls it was impossible to see more than a few feet ahead.

When the fog was thickest, I would jump inside it looking for answers, thinking maybe I could fly through the mist. I was the little abandoned man who had to look out for himself. Momentarily the fog freed me from captivity when I could not see the confining walls of what was now a monastery on the southwestern border of China and Nepal. During that time I ceased to feel like the criminal who had committed no crime and had no idea where he was being held.

Looking back, it is a wonder I survived the first months in the monastery. There was no psychosis motivating my destructive behavior, it was pure rage which, in the final analysis, probably prevented me from going insane. It provided an outlet when I knew of no other. I kicked and bit every boy and man whenever they got within range. It was useless to try and break things as I had done at school in London because I could find nothing in the monastery that would break. It gave me a sense of accomplishment that everyone seemed to fear me and most of them had the marks of my violence to remind them of why. When they tried to discipline me for my bad behavior, it took four of them to hold me down while Wbiso struck me with his bamboo gong stick. The irony was, of course, that from a very early age I had become immune to physical punishment.

"You must be good!" Wbiso shrieked as he struck me again and again. The only result was that the little man got marked in my brain as public enemy number one and he bloody well knew it. Everyone else knew their danger as well as I kept on kicking and biting, the two most dangerous weapons in my arsenal. It took me quite a while to realize that although I never held back, they did. I was as cruel as I could imagine, but they were not. I wanted them all to die, but they wanted me to learn calmness and peace. The more I hated, the more they showed me love and kindness. There was nothing in my history that prepared me for that kind of response.

My prison was not merely the four walls of that foreboding citadel, it was the anxieties and the things I missed. I wanted Grandmother, and Shahla, and Hailie. I wanted the green playing fields of Manchester and the stolen rides on the double-decker and making fun of the conductor. I wanted the cookies Hailie used to give me so much I could actually smell them. I just wanted to be a kid and go to school, and I wanted to be far away from the monastery.

There are only two mistakes
one can make along the road
to truth—not going all the
way, and not starting.

My journey toward truth was far from commencing as I sat on the tree stump in the middle of the monastery and gazed up at the stars, the galaxies I named, the objects that became my only friends. They were all I had to substitute for the shreds of the golden football Hailie had given me with her love and Father had denied me with his cold-hearted hate. I played at trying to move the stars around and screamed with delight whenever I saw a meteor streaking across the black velvet sky. For that time, the sky was my private soccer field, but it did not ease my loneliness.

Not once, however, did I shed a tear for all that had been ripped out of my life like a mighty wind uproots a giant tree, leaving a black void in the earth. Nor did I hope—there was nothing to hope for. I participated in daily life with the other boys, doing chores, not a monk but living like one. But at night I escaped to my tree stump and watched my friends, the stars. It was during those quiet times that my imagination kicked in. The London fog rolls around me as I steal a bus ride—"Lad did you crawl under the turnstile?" the conductor demands—I smile and take a seat. "You should do it," I say to Hailie. "Michael, that's cheating!" she says. But I don't care. It's fun to get one over on the conductor who keeps looking at me but says nothing else. "Hailie, do you have any cookies?" I ask.

> *Deny thy might by looking at*
> *the mountains or listening to*
> *the sounds of the starry sky.*

Pure evil had banished me here after the longest trip of my life to a place with no name and not even a dot on any map. Now I wonder what karma the gentle monks and boys felt must have inflicted me on them. I had been brought to stand before the Master of the monastery, an old man with a gentle voice and a benign smile. He put his hands together and bowed respectfully in a gesture meant to please me, but on the contrary it only irritated my troubled heart. My mind was racing with questions: What is this place? Why am I here? I don't want to be here! Who are you people?

"Me Ouiyen," the old man said, still smiling, "Good. Good."

His pidgin English irritated me further . . . he was standing too close . . . my foot moved like lightning and caught him in the groin, totally unprotected in those loose, cotton robes. He fell to his knees, unable to speak, only able to wave for other monks to come and help him. Everyone was horrified, but I was having the time of my life thinking to myself that nobody in this place I never asked to visit would be safe. That was all I could think of at that moment unable to identify even to myself. Then I recalled something Grandmother had told me, "Michael, God will never give you more than you can handle." In my heart, I railed at God, "I wish you didn't trust me so much!"

Master Ouiyen issued an order that I was to be treated with the greatest respect and no violence or punishment should be used on me. That became my ticket to inflict pain right and left without fear of reprisal. They tried to get close to me, to be my friends, but getting close to me was asking for it. It did not take long for those men and boys to realize that treating me with kindness simply was not going to work.

Although I was unaware of Master Ouiyen's repeal of his previous order, I soon found out when I finally discovered some breakable dishes and gave another monk a bruised eye. Four large monks surrounded me, and one of them held me down on the ground by simply applying pressure to the nerve in my lower back while the other three stuffed me into a large potato sack. Unceremoniously, the monks then carried me into the corral that housed the largest, smelliest ox I had ever seen. Dumping me there like so much garbage, they went out, locking the gate behind them. After struggling out of the sack, I attempted to open the gate to no avail as I cursed and screamed, calling them all kinds of names which I'm sure none of them understood. It was impossible for me to scale the high, slick stone walls of the ox pen. As I calmed down gradually, I glared at the only living thing inside that manure-scented enclosure, the huge ox that probably wondered what sort of animal had been introduced into its heretofore private domain. In a rush of rage, I ran to the backside of the ox and kicked it as hard as I could. It did not phase the ox, but it felt to me like kicking the stone wall, and I actually cried from the pain in my foot. Limping in tears over to the wall, I sat down and watched the ox continue to eat and switch flies with its rope-like tail.

I think that was the beginning of a kind of mutual respect that developed between the ox and me, for I was to be locked up with him many times for my bad behavior. I had learned the hard way that I did not want to mess with that gigantic beast, and he was content to allow me to keep my distance. While I watched the animal eat his grain pacifically, I fumed within my very being that I could not—would not—allow those monks to break the invincible kid. I had plenty of occasions to meditate on that resolve.

You will not be punished for
your anger; you will be
punished by your anger.

The level of the punishments within the ox pen increased as the monks often came in and tied my hands making me feel like an old boxer photographed with his boxing gloves on as though to express who he was. The punishment of the monks inside that odiferous place was not painful physically, but it was humiliating and began taking the fight out of me. What was the use? In that enclosure, I was only one small boy with his hands tied against four very large and very strong monks who had learned to protect themselves from my kicks and bites. They held me down in that vile combination of mud and excrement, often rubbing my face in the filth, walking on my back to make it hard for me to breathe. Gradually they were breaking me down, but I was not ever really broken.

It was during one of those humiliating bouts with the large monks, when my face and body were muddied by the ox's filth, that I heard a loud voice calling, "What are you doing? Stop at once!" The ones holding me down froze in place and removed their hands from my person. A very large hand reached down and pulled me up from the dirt and degradation, loosened my bonds, and began cleaning off my face gently. Reflexively, I smacked the large monk so hard in the face that it brought a shower of tears to his eyes, but he did not stop cleaning me or speaking softly to me. Nevertheless, I pulled away from his grasp and ran to the open gate of the ox pen and dashed all the way across the monstrous fort to the far wall where there was a collection of stone carvings kept out of the way. Up on a stone platform were carving of two lions wearing crown that suddenly reminded me of Dookie. When the other boys crept close enough to see what I was doing, they broke out laughing to see me there talking to this lion's head. I cared not because I knew they were too frightened to come any closer to the angry boy who had the jaw of a lion. In that vast enclosure, partially carved out of the side of a cliff with four containing walls around and cold gray skies above, there stood a nine-year-old boy coping with a cruel exile by conversing with the ghost of his pet rooster.

PART III

THE MONKS

CHAPTER NINE

POWER OF THE GENTLE SPIRIT

BUDDHISM, PER SE, NEITHER CONFIRMS NOR DENIES the existence of the supernatural (God, Demons, Heavens, Hells, etc.). However, monks employ deities and celestial protectors in their practices, but these are generally considered to be emanations of the mediator's own mind and thus not fundamentally real.

It seems at first that they are not of this world, these monks living out their lives of mountain seclusion. They glide purposefully as if on some devout mission from on high through the monastery. At times, they flit by at great speed, their brown tunics and brown robes swishing as they pass, pausing only briefly to bow reverently in the direction of the shrine.

They seemed to float just above the surface of the ground, those older monks who went about their daily chores in silence and serenity. Although I did not realize it at the time, those men and boys existed on an inner strength that had nothing to do with an ability to inflict pain. Looking back, I find it utterly amazing that they could year after year survive the harshness of their surroundings while maintaining an aura of calm serenity. At first, I thought about that equanimity of spirit as a kind of weakness. Nothing could have been further from the truth.

The clothing they wore, robes made of thin fabric they wound around themselves in a special way, hardly seemed to me as any kind of protection from the vicious elements engulfing the monastery. The monastery itself was simply the ruins of a long abandoned fortress to which they had claimed squatter's rights. When the snow fell outside, it came down inside as well except for the few places where they had put up makeshift shelters in the sleeping quarters, the kitchen, and the library. In addition to the covered areas, there was the ox pen, garden area, and an empty space I would later transform into a playing field.

Day in and day out, the monks rose early in the morning to perform their prayers before beginning their day's chores. Life in the monastery was one of regular routine carried out almost in silence. Civility was of utmost importance as they greeted each other in passing, bowing out of respect for the other person. To me, at the time I first arrived, the whole scene was ridiculous. Why did they stay here? Why did they not go out and get a life? What was wrong with them?

Almost immediately I learned about the hierarchy inside the monastery. Age seemed to me to be one of the main requisites for status. Older monks were treated with deference, something that was foreign to me since (except for my grandmother) I still saw all adults as the enemy. Then there was the importance place on certain job functions such as Wbiso, the gong ringer. At the top of the hierarchy was, of course, the abbot or Ouiyen. In this monastery that was Master Kyi, the man whose introduction to me was my foot in his groin.

Ouiyen Kyi was a Burmese monk whose Chinese name was He-Ping, meaning peaceful and calm. The name suited him well, though his restraint around me made me at first believe that he was soft and ineffectual. He spoke so softly I had to strain to hear him, and he spoke so slowly that it seemed to be an eternity before he got everything out he wanted to say. No one dared interrupt him when he spoke.

Our Ouiyen considered each individual in our nameless monastery with the greatest respect, calling each man and boy by his name. Although Ouiyen Kyi was a short man, he was incredibly well built and very strong. It took me a long time to realize that a man with such massively muscled arms and shoulders could have decked me that day when we met and I kicked him in the groin. And it took a much longer time for me to figure out why he hadn't.

The fact of the matter is that I could not really understand how this group of men and boys could exist in such an unfriendly environment. Given my choice of any place on earth to live, this one wouldn't have made it into the top 10,000. It looked far more like a prison than it did a domicile. The work they did each day was back breaking labor, tending the rice paddies and caring for the fruit trees in and around the monastery. And the silence was deafening.

Yet if there is one word that comes to mind when I think back on those strange men and boys it would be this: peace. Even with the one-boy wrecking crew in their midst, the entire group maintained an equanimity of spirit that was completely beyond my comprehension. In the outside world the title of "gentleman" refers to a kind of refinement born of education and sophistication. These men were gentle, not gentile. They were kind, not artificially tactful. No one railed against the fate that had brought them there to utter isolation and the travail of mere existence. They were actually grateful for what I saw as degradation but to them was bountiful blessing.

I saw them withstand the elements and trudge up the mountainside to a special place of prayer and meditation filled with song and praise. In spite of the rocks, boulders, and weather, which were never completely comfortable, these monks taught me by example, even when I had no idea I was being taught.

The diet of the monks was simple without the spices and presentation I had become accustomed to in my earlier life. It was food they raised through the work of their own hands, completely unaware of the idea of a supermarket. They planted, harvested, and prepared the food themselves. There was no gluttony in the monastery but rather a spirit of sharing that amazed me. It was as though they were completely oblivious to the difficulties of their lives, caring for others before taking thought of themselves.

It was years after I finally left the monastery that I began to appreciate the saintliness of those dedicated monks. By contrast with the so-called civilized world with its avarice and greed, its hedonistic self-indulgence, I learned to appreciate the purity of the monks who nurtured me back to life. The Fat Man may have been right. I could have ended up on the gallows had I not been banished to a community filled with love and patience.

PART IV

KAKO

CHAPTER TEN

THE IMMOVABLE OBJECT

"Hatred does not cease by hatred, but only by love;
this is the eternal rule".

FOR THOUSANDS OF YEARS MAN HAS PONDERED THE impossible meeting of the immovable object and the irresistible force, a coming together of such power that nothing can be moved or destroyed. In the first nine years of my existence, I had become a kind of irresistible force that moved every object in my path through the force of my rage. I was about to meet my immovable object.

"I want to be your friend," I heard a voice say in almost perfect English and I looked up into the face of the man who had tried to clean my face in the ox pen.

His face was beautiful, bejeweled with the largest brown eyes, and his complexion was tanned from exposure to the sun as he worked outside the monastery. Looking at me kindly from those remarkable eyes, he got down on his knees so as not to tower over me. His glowing face was the perfect target for my kick that landed squarely on his brilliant teeth. My kick was so hard that I actually hurt my foot so bad that blood poured from my toes just as it was running from his face. What happened next confused me for being so out of the ordinary, for becoming the one immovable object that did not cower or recoil from my violence.

"I'm sorry. I'm so sorry," he said, less intelligibly because of the blood collecting in his mouth and running down his chin. He ignored his own injury and began wiping the red flow from my toes and leg. "Does your foot hurt?" he asked.

"You bloody bastard!" I screamed and jerked my injured foot away from him and ran away leaving him there on his knees. There was no remorse in me, but his reaction and kindness were not in the realm of my experience. I understood the beatings and being dumped into the disgusting, smelly ox pen; but I did not understand kindness aimed at turning away wrath.

When I saw him again that afternoon, he was putting something down on paper. As I approached, he handed the paper to me and said, "I made this for you." It was a drawing of a boy with wings, the sun above his head, and many heads down below bowing down to the flying boy. "I am going to call you Shiniwa, the Living, Burning Sun," he said pointing to the picture, "This is who you are. I want to be your friend." He sat across from me, his body wide open, and I had the urge to hit him again, to inflict more pain on his terribly swollen face.

"My name is Kako," he said softly, "I have been here all my life. I came here many years ago much like you did, only I was much younger than you when I was left here for the monks to care for. I cannot say how you feel, but I can say I know it is not easy." He was feeling around in his mind for the right words, speaking slowly and thoughtfully. "I only heard about you three days ago," he continued, "That is how long it took me to get here. I came as soon as I heard."

The urge to strike him left me like geese flying from a pond. The irresistible force had met his immovable object, and I sat down to listen to him. From that moment, my life changed. Kako was always nearby and no one dared to disturb or ridicule me in any way. His presence only a few feet away from me at all times was the first real security I had ever experienced in my life.

Three things cannot be long hidden:
the sun, the moon, and the truth.

There was no formal schooling in the monastery, but that is not to say that there was no education. With Kako there beside me, I began to really observe what was going on inside those huge rock walls. The monks had their daily routines of chores; each was responsible for tending the fruit trees or the gardens and rice paddies around the fort. I really noticed for the first time how they greeted each other with polite bows and very little verbal communication. It did not escape me that they helped each other without expectation of reward or reciprocation. Everyone in the monastery wore the same orange or brown robes and sandals, now including even me because the clothes I came with were outgrown and threadbare. I can testify that clothes do not make the man, for though I dressed as a monk, I was most definitely not one.

As I calmed somewhat—do not think my transformation was instantaneous—I returned to my former interests and fashioned a football out of cloth strips. Kako looked at it asked what it was. He said nothing after I explained what the lump of cloth was intended for. A couple of days later, he came to me with a ball made of bamboo and coconut skin, all held together with strips from the gum tree. It was the best ball I had ever owned and brought hours of pleasure to me as I manipulated it with my feet, knees, chest, and head. To give a better idea of how large the fortress was that now housed a monastery, there was an area just behind the dining area that was almost as large as a regulation football field that became my playground and once again I had excited spectators watching me from the sidelines.

Kako became much more than my teacher. He was the father I never had, a confidant to whom I could reveal my mind, my soul. We talked about Shahla and my pain at seeing her waste away. We talked about Hailie and the cookies she brought me and our happy time at her family's estate in Wales. We talked about Dookie and how he was murdered to hurt me. And we talked about Grandmother, the woman with wise words like Kako's.

"Would you like to see the river?" Kako asked me one day.

"There's no river here, you stupid bald bastard," I snapped, thinking he did not understand my colorful vocabulary.

"Not here, out there is a river," he said, taking no umbrage at my foul comment. He was pointing at the huge gate that closed over the drawbridge. "Out there," he said again, "We go tomorrow if Shiniwa wants to go."

For longest time the only thing I saw from outside was the sky above and the odd glimpse of the horizon when the monks were briefly let out the big gate to tend their gardens and rice paddies. My world had literally been confined to these four unscalable walls. Did I want to see outside was the mother of all rhetorical questions. So early the next morning, the gates were opened and the monster drawbridge was lowered for Kako and me to walk out into the open spaces.

It was a short hike to the river just beyond the northern wall of the monastery. It was small and crystal clear and I was so excited I looked at Kako and asked, "Can we call it the Thames River?"

"No," he replied, "we will call it the SHOG River."

"SHOG River!" I shouted, "What kind of stupid name is that?"

Kako smiled, "S for Shahla, H for Hailie, O for Dookie, and G for Grandmother. The River SHOG."

I was speechless. A river named for all the people I loved most dearly! It was brilliant! And Kako grinned as though he had made a hat trick score.

There was a thick and verdant forest on the opposite side of the river filled with monkeys and all sorts of birds singing their songs of Mother Nature. We were able to cross over and Kako took me to a place beneath a huge apple tree, telling me it was his favorite spot in the forest. He sat down with his back to the tree as I climbed up high into its branches. When I got as far as I could go, there was a brilliant red apple just within my reach, but the moment I touched the luscious fruit, the Devil came out in me again. Without thinking, I hurled the apple downward, striking Kako on the head so hard it raised an ugly bump. He didn't flinch or even look up to see where the apple had come from. When I got down out of the tree, I noticed the lump on his head but made no mention of what I had just done. I started walking away and Kako got up to follow me. We walked in the forest for hours until I complained that I was hungry. Without a word, he reached into his robes and pulled out the apple that was all smashed and bloody on one side and handed it to me.

"Are you crazy?" I shouted, "I'm not going to eat that bloody mess."

"It was a delicious apple before you decided to destroy it by throwing it at me," Kako said matter-of-factly in his soft voice.

I just stopped in my tracks and stared at him. The object lesson was much more effective than the gong ringer's stick.

"All that we are is the result of what we have thought. If a man speaks or acts with an evil thought, pain follows him. If a man speaks or acts with a pure thought, happiness follows him, like a shadow that never leaves him. To enjoy good health, to bring true happiness to one's life, to bring peace to your mind, one must first discipline and control one's own mind. If a man can control his mind he can find the way to enlightenment, and all wisdom and virtue will naturally come to him," Kako taught. My lessons had begun.

What is education? From my personal point of view, perhaps somewhere along the line of school books and whiteboards, perhaps the real essence of education has become obliterated by formality and conformity. My education came from Kako, my schoolroom an apple tree, and my curriculum, perhaps unorthodox but highly effective. Kako taught me how to cook, a skill overlooked in a macho oriented culture where the basic survival need of preparing food is left entirely up to the females of the species. Obviously, there were no females in the monastery.

"Tell me about yourself Kako". I asked my mentor as we were settling under the apple tree.

It was a beautiful autumn morning. It was an exceptionally cold morning. I had running nose and a silent constant cough I could not get over. There was not enough heat in my quarter. Our hands and feet were always ice cold. I had somehow adjusted to the harsh climate but the cold nights and unforgiving wind were always intolerable. The monastery did not have interior walls rather manmade partitioned wooden dividers that held no heat or resistance to the howling winds.

I left to stay in Luery monastery for a few years when I was much younger. Kako said. Luery monastery is the closest shrine to this place. Master Ouiyen wanted me to go there since there were more opportunities to receive better educations and exposures to the outside world.

I studied under an old English missionary who mentored me through all the modern educations. He was a gifted and exceptionally knowledgeable man. He had lost his wife and his two daughters in a car accident in Malaysia. He had then moved to the area directly outside of Luery in search of peace and tranquility. He had become a true asset to the monastery as he had provided them a treasury of books and educational resources. I truly enjoyed my time with him. He suddenly left leaving me quite undecided about my future and studies.

I continued my studies in modern education with a German textile trader who lived a short distance from the monastery. He passed away about a year later when he felt very sick.

I stayed at Luery monastery for a few years more studying under Master He-Ping. He trained me as well as Master Ouiyen Kyi.

I used to travel between the two monasteries quite often. I was planning to settle in Luery per master Kyi orders until I heard about you.

Master Ouiyen had dispatched someone to come and summon me from Luery. I did not know anything about you when the messenger arrived. He told me that you were stronger than the ox and wilder than the mountain wind. I am glad I came. My mentor said smiling.

"Life is a clock with hands moving in
the direction of your destiny".

Whether it was stroke of luck or God's will, which I take the latter, I rode the cart of the heaven port.

Kako never talked again about his time in Luery, but he kept in his quarter a small green color rope that the German textile man had given him. There was a small writing on it. It read; "I learnt more as your teacher than an old man. Haans".

Kako taught me to become a warrior, not to become aggressive but to become a man of reason. I believe he literally taught me everything he knew over the period of the next few years. He talked, I listened. How different it was from the way I had behaved in Mrs. Foresstes' classroom back in England where my mind was too occupied with the next havoc I could create to pay much attention in class. From the library inside the monastery, Kako selected many books that I had to carry as we set out for our classroom under the apple tree. I had to write down everything he said and keep a daily journal. At the time I was not aware of the scope of the education Kako was giving me. I had to pay attention because he would very often stop and quiz me on what he had just said. It became quite a game for me to be able to repeat his instruction on those occasions. He also taught me how to memorize a chapter in just a few minutes and be able to answer his questions on the material.

Mathematics was drilled into me by piling literally hundreds of smooth river rocks along the banks. Our physics lab was the kitchen of the monastery. The nearby lake became our chemistry lab, and the trees in the forest served to teach me algorithms. Physical education classes consisted of hard physical labor for a few hours every day. The world was my classroom and there was no principal's office for me to visit when I misbehaved.

As exciting as my education became, and as close as my friendship with Kako developed, I still had my resentments and disappointments. I still felt trapped in a prison, an exile not of my own making. Fortunately there was Kako to hear my complaints, and there were plenty of those:

"I'm forgetting my sister's face!"

"I have nothing in this place! They sent me here with nothing!"

"I don't know who I am anymore!"

"Does it mean that I have to live here like the rest of you all my life?"

"What if I want to leave one day?"

"I'm not a criminal and this is no prison! Why do I have to stay here?"

"Why do they all hate me [in the monastery]? I hate them back!"

My complaining elicited an entirely new result that in itself was an object lesson that took me some time to learn. Kako never commented on my beefs, but he listened. I mean really listened, as I was to understand later. He made himself my sounding board, let me get my frustrations off my chest, without moral comment or lecturing advice. Grandmother used to listen to me in the same way, I recalled.

Not all of Kako's lessons made much sense to me at first, I'll have to admit. A few days after I had dumped all my resentful and confused feelings on him, he gave me some instructions that no one else on earth would have dared present to me. "Sit on your knees," he said, "Bring your hands together and drop your face into your hands keeping your eyes closed." What is this? I thought, but he was Kako, my only friend and constant companion, so I did what he told me to do.

"Now, listen to yourself," he continued in his soft voice, "Hear nothing from the outside world, it does not exist. Just listen deep within yourself." There were a few moments of pause before he continued, "Now, without moving your position, lift your inner self up from the two of us and look down at us from above."

Was he crazy? My skepticism rose to an all time high, as I attempted to follow his directions.

"Sweep at our faces and pass through our bodies as you fly," he went on, "Talk to me from above. See yourself across your physical body, your soul above looking down."

I don't want to make it sound like some kind of miracle that Kako was eventually able to teach me how to lift myself out of my body and see myself as I looked down from above, but I was able to do it. It was the beginning of the spiritual lessons Kako would teach me over the next few years.

Those lessons were not meaningless exercises in meditation. They were valuable life lessons that began helping me overcome my monsters, to control my dreams and banish the nightmares that had plagued me for years. The control, he told me, was to master my own life and cease trying to go down closed highways. "Party with your life," he said, "dance with your soul, and mate with your thoughts." He was shaping and polishing my troubled inner soul, helping me to find what I never knew I had. I was learning how to forget and why to forgive as he patiently answered and reshaped the immature and childish comments I made during our studies in spirituality.

There was no part of my troubled past that Kako tiptoed around, including giving me a whole new prospective of my father. "Be just in your judgment of your father," Kako said during one of my meditations, "To do that you must enter into his mind and find his deeds and leave if you see his intentions are pure and at peace. See how he does not see himself as one of the wicked people who commit crimes like those who lie, abuse, gossip, steal, and act lasciviously. Make such things the objects of your disbelief."

I must comment that while Kako was able to help me temper the flames that had burned so long inside my gut, he was never able to erase the scars of Dookie, my mutilated sister, the tatters of my golden football, nor (as I was to learn years later) how he caused my beloved grandmother to grieve herself to death.

Still his words slowly had a profound effect on me, "Shiniwa, every human is the author of his own health or disease. You are not the hermit desiring the path of truth by climbing mountains of swords or throwing yourself into the risks of the path edged with the perils of the sword, mountains bristling with selfishness, and stoking the fires of hatred. In the end, you would find your struggles only in worldly passions.

"Happiness, my friend, is a delusion, a base passion of emotion and confused values. To live a pure and unselfish life, one must count nothing as one's own in the very midst of abundance."

It took years of these sessions with Kako for the lessons to really sink in, to understand what these wise and precious words actually meant. I had come there walking a path of inner conflict more rugged than the painful rocks I had crossed to get to the monastery. Now I was eating apples from ghostly trees and sitting in impossible fields of flowers elevated by words of wisdom and deep spiritual thoughts. That is not a metamorphosis that happens overnight.

I still had a stubborn streak a mile long inside me which came out every now and again when Kako tried to get me involved in my own spiritual growth. One day in particular I remember as though it were yesterday.

"What are you thinking?" Kako asked as he walked up to where I sat under the big apple tree.

"Nothing," I said in a surly retort, "I'm thinking of nothing."

"Then you're not living," he said, "You breathe thinking. When you do not think, you are sleeping. Sleep is a kind of death that comes over us when our eyes are closed in peace. That is the time when we dream, and our dreams are the things we think when we are awake. In other words, awake, you think what you want to think and in sleep you dream what you want to dream."

Yeah, right, I thought, like I want to dream about Dookie, or Shahla, or all those other nightmares that wake me up screaming.

"I am NOT thinking!" I insisted.

Kako never argued with me. He never judged or condemned. He would always come up with something to make me focus my thoughts, even when I maintained that I had no thoughts at all. He took my right hand and asked, "Shiniwa, can you feel my hand?"

"Yes."

"Good. Then close your eyes."

I did. Then he removed his big hand and replaced it with an object that was cool and small. I clutched it, feeling it with my fingers. It was round and hard and rough on the surface. I began to form an image of a rock in my mind. I figured out that its calloused surface was pitted with small holes. Ha! I was satisfied I knew what it was.

"What is it?" I asked, eyes still closed, but confident I already knew the answer.

There was no reply from Kako.

Okay. So maybe this is some kind of trick, and there's more I should be able to understand from feeling this thing I held in my right hand.

"What is it?" I asked again in a little more demanding tone of voice.

Silence.

I opened my eyes and found myself alone under the apple tree with Kako nowhere in sight. I looked at my hand and, sure enough, I found a small black rock, pitted with many holes. I understood that

Kako had directed my thinking toward solving a problem on my own, a method he often used in his teaching.

My curiosity now stimulated, I looked again at the small volcanic rock and began trying to count the number of small holes on its surface. So engrossed I was in counting the number of holes in that rock that I spent the whole of the afternoon counting again and again, coming up with a different number every time. It was frustrating as well as challenging, and never being one to back away from a challenge, I counted and recounted trying to come up with a definitive answer to the question of how many holes are in the rock—62, no, wait, 63.

In fact, the next time I saw Kako, that was his first question, "How many holes are in the rock, Shiniwa?"

"The answer is 64, right?"

He never answered that question. Years later, it would come to me that a major weakness in western education practice is filling students' heads with encyclopedias of information, teaching them what to think instead of teaching them how to think. Kako's next question sent me off on another mental exercise, "Which hole is largest and which is smallest?"

Included in my lesson on thought was the inevitable spiritual value Kako always added to the mix. "Life," he said, "is a treadmill. Only the lucky ones ever get off. Unless one alters his way of looking at life, it is stagnant like simply going through the motions without understanding."

Speaking of stagnant, that was the way I viewed the monastery. It was a monument to routine and as quiet as a tomb. The monks worked in silence only speaking very softly when it was necessary. I imagined it as a world where the language was deadly silence.

CHAPTER ELEVEN

A DRAWING FROM THE HEART OF SHINIWA

KAKO COULD ALWAYS FIND WAYS TO GET ME TO communicate my feelings, even when the words could not be dragged out of me. One day he surprised me with a simple request, "Shiniwa, draw me a picture."

"Of what?" I replied.

"Whatever you want," he said.

I was somewhere in my twelfth year when he made that request of me, and, looking back, I wonder if he knew that his request would produce an image of my mental and emotional state of mind. What, I wonder now, had he expected to see when I finished my masterpiece—an apple tree? A bird? A mountain vista? Of course, I shall never really know the answer to that question. What I do know is that Kako was both surprised and touched by the drawing I handed him—a rooster with a funny crown, a football, and two girls. After looking at my drawing, he turned his face away like he always did when he did not want me to see the tears in his eyes. Later, I observed that he had pinned that drawing on the wall at the head of his bed where it remained until his death.

Let us talk about outside world. Kako said to my surprise.

He had never talked about that subject before. I had forgotten about it and it really did not matter anymore. I was not going back there.

I had everything I needed within those walls. I do not know if it was contempt or surrender, but I had finally accepted living my life within those cold rugged plateaus.

I had abandoned hope. Here, monastery had given me a sanctuary and refuge.

Those who exiled me to this monastery had forced their relentlessness way of their lives on me. I had finally found peace and I was not giving it up.

Why do I need to know anything about the outside world?

What would the world offer me anymore?

Why should the world know that I was there?

This is the same world that I learned earlier in my life that cruelty and greed were the principle codes.

> *To gild refined gold, to paint the lily,*
> *To throw a perfume on the violet.*

What is so worthy of this world known to those worldlier citizens that a pebble thrown ends it?

The world I knew sat on needles and drank the blood of its own.

Outside world, isn't it the same place where the governments sell peace under the days' market names?

Where families trade their young ones for money?

And the officials put a rope around your neck letting you breath better?

Why do I want to know about outside world?

I like it here. I said.

I think I know enough about the outside world. I have no intention of going back. I said agitatedly.

I need to tell you more and train you about it. You will go back one day. You must know what I know. Kako persisted. It was the beginning of a dreadful lesson.

CHAPTER TWELVE

A TURNING POINT

OUT OF THE BLUE ONE AFTERNOON I ASKED KAKO, "DO you know how to play football?"

"No, Shiniwa."

"Would you like to learn?"

"Of course, Shiniwa," he replied in a dubious tone.

The next day on our walk, I took along my prized homemade bamboo ball and began explaining the rules of the game to Kako. He hitched up his robe so that he could run and made me laugh at how funny he looked doing it. I did all sorts of things with the ball to make him look stupid, sending the ball between his legs and jogging it all around him as he labored to keep his eye on the fast moving object. I admired his persistence, how he never stopped trying, and we laughed a great deal as we shared something of my life experience together.

On our way back to the monastery that day, I asked Kako if he thought we could put together a soccer team. He looked deeply into my eyes and nodded, but then he added, "One condition, Shiniwa. Be kind. Follow your heart." I knew why he said that to me. True, I was much calmer now and had learned a lot from him, but the ember was still there, buried deep to be sure, but there nonetheless. I still recalled the pain I had often inflicted on others on the football field without, however, the least bit of remorse.

Michael had risen once again! I was captain, coach, and referee, teaching football in a place the world knows nothing about to people who knew nothing about the world. In a flash I had recruited more players than I needed and in spite of some resistance within the monastery itself to monks running and playing, chasing a ball made of bamboo strips.

Once I had the monks trained and the games started, however, the entire population of the monastery came out in force to watch and cheer as we played. This was better than prayers. This was Shiniwa's game.

It is hard to imagine; and if I hadn't lived it myself, I probably would never have believed it—a soccer field inside an ancient fort with monks running up and down, their robes hitched up for play, and having the time of their lives. Just the idea of a soccer game in that hostile environment where at times, when the snows fell, the entire field became a blanket of white, is almost beyond credibility. Nevertheless, that is what happened when at least one of the loves of my past life was restored to me.

Snow on the ground of the fort-monastery was a common occurrence situated there as it was in the Himalayas, but more uncomfortable than that were the ice water baths that had to be endured on a daily basis. Here again, however, was another chance for me to send shockwaves through the place when my disregard for modesty at the bath raised eyebrows until I turned it into a post-game locker room with two teams of sweaty soccer players. The monks kept an orange sarong-like garment wrapped around their waists as they poured the frigid water over their heads and bodies. Once they were thoroughly bathed, they covered themselves with a clean, dry robe and removed the sodden garment underneath. It was a ritual I was never able to master.

Our games were not any less rough than the game I once played in Wales and got red carded for unnecessary contact. I used every psychological trick in the book to intimidate the opposing team, giving them that famous Michael stare that might have caused them to wet their pants—if they had been wearing pants. I kicked the opponents as hard as I could and it was all legal because I was the one who set the rules backed up by my wild card by the name of Kako. The football playing monks were up to the challenge, and as for me, it was my show and the first real pleasure I had at the monastery.

Soccer never interfered with my education, though, and I still went out to my school under the sky with Kako. The more I learned from him, the more I wanted to learn about him. So, one day I asked him, "Why did you become a monk?"

"I am told the old master found me as an infant in a small straw basket just outside of this monastery. He named me Kako. It means a gift. He raised me as his own son," Kako said. "I have been here all my life. The master taught me everything I know. We also have all those books that I have read over many times. I wish we had more books. There are a lot more books in the Luery Monastery."

"Where is that?" I asked.

"It's about a three-day walk from here, Shiniwa, so we don't go there but once every few years. We go as a group on that long journey but, of course, we can never visit there as often as we'd like."

My next question was really stupid, "Did you know your grandmother, Kako?"

"No, Shiniwa, I never knew where I came from. The only family I ever had were the old master who took me in and the other monks here in the monastery. This place, these people, you, the old apple tree—these are my family. When I die I want my ashes buried by this tree." I noticed his hands were trembling as he spoke. "You changed my life, Shiniwa," he said, "I want to thank you for that. You are the fire in my life and the fire that I saw." He sat next to me under the tree.

"Are you crying?" I asked, noticing that his round cheeks were wet. His eyes flooded with tears, his strong shoulders drooped. He brought his hands together and bowed his head, praying. Of course, I didn't interrupt his prayers, but I was a little confused as to what exactly had transpired between us that afternoon. It was not until some years later that I got the full significance of Kako's conversation.

> *"Place not a valuable on a curved surface, for thieves holiday bags are open for it to fall in".*

Kako sat down, wrapping his robes gracefully around his legs, and called me to come sit with him. He began to speak, "Love, Shiniwa, is kindness, and passion is a crime. No punishment will ever come for love. Life in itself is no mystery. Set your expectations, welcome change, and accept your fate. You own a miracle, the health that is in your body. Let your soul guard your purity and your health guard your body as you travel through life. The secret of health for both mind and body is not to mourn for the past, nor to worry about the future, but to live the present moment wisely and earnestly." This preamble led up to a question Kako was about to raise in the style of Socrates. I remember it sounding like a movie script:

Kako: What is the most difficult thing in the world to do?
Shiniwa: To be a monk?
Kako: You are Shiniwa. You're not a monk.

Shiniwa: To be a Buddhist?

Kako: You are not Buddhist. You believe what you want to believe.

Shiniwa: Maybe going back home?

Kako: Maybe.

Shiniwa: To walk with my sister along the Thames?

Kako: You walk with her in your heart every day.

Shiniwa: To touch my grandmother's face?

Kako: Close your eyes. She is sitting right next to you.

Shiniwa: To see Hailie and eat her cookies?

Kako: When you walk, her memories walk along side you.

Shiniwa: Riding on Dookie?

Kako: Is that why you sometimes call me Dookie?

Shiniwa: To burn my father with really hot fire?

Kako: No, Shiniwa, son, no!

Shiniwa: To be the best football player in the world?

Kako: You are a champion at heart, Shiniwa, you have magical feet.

Shiniwa: To lock my father into a concrete cell?

Kako: [Silence!]

I wasn't silent, however. I kept rambling on about things I thought might be the most difficult in the world to do. I guess to shut me up, he offered me a piece of bread he had baked that morning. When I was finally quiet, Kako continued, "Simple life, having a simple life is the most difficult thing to do! Imagine, living in a society where money and greed is the lord of the land. Your appearance influences your surroundings. You have to meet the demands of a failed society. Your wealth talks and your silence is buried. You undertake to create your own image which is all that defines your position in the community. You become only a made up image, and not your true self."

I had just been given another spoonful of spirituality. I was to get another dose when one day I made a disparaging comment about another person.

There was an old farmer, who lived between the two very small, sparsely populated villages closest to the monastery and were the only outside contact for the monks. We were not allowed to ask for anything from the villagers and had strict orders of silence whenever we came in contact with them.

The old farmer lived in a ramshackle and faded green and blue wooden house. I always saw him walking behind an old mule dragging a huge rotten fork digging into the wet soil drowned by the melting snow from the mountains. For an old man, he seemed exceptionally energetic as he followed and yelled at the mule all day long. I think the mule had a deaf ear to him as he would pace the same never look back. The old man never wore a shirt but had a big round domed straw hat held in place by a strap under his chin and (I guess this is what irritated me about him the most) he would always pause and stare at me as I walked past. His stare never made me feel that I could converse with him or be his friend, so even when he waved a greeting at me, I would ignore him as I went past. He would return to his task and sing old Buddhist hymns as he trudged along:

> *May the rising of spirits,*
> *Those whom you remembered*
> *and loved,*
> *Come to the mind and behold.*

You shall forever long, as one
who sees,
Let the spirits rise.

"Why do you ignore the old man?" Kako asked me one day as we walked by the farm.

"I don't like him," I said, frowning, "He looks weird. I think he must be crazy walking behind that old black mule and singing every day. That thing is not something I want to look at."

Right away I knew I had put my foot in it. The look of anguish and pain that crossed Kako's face spoke volumes. My harsh words about an old man I didn't even know had broken Kako's heart hearing my old arrogance come to the surface, brushing aside all the spiritual things Kako had taught me about life and dealing with other people. I was stricken by how easy it was for me to inflict pain on the one person I could call my friend. Still, on that day I was more Michael than Shiniwa, and the old resentments and pain inured me to any pain I might be inflicting on Kako.

In his soft voice, Kako admonished, "That thing as you call him has a name, Shiniwa. His name is Mdogho and he has been working that little farm as long as I can remember. He gives what he grows on his farm to villagers who are in need and his humble door is always open to everyone, domestic or foreign, no questions asked. Once he lost an eye doing his hard work, but that never stopped him from serving his community and being a source of protection and aid for those in need. Mdogho is a dignified and respected man." Kako's voice trailed off as he stared at lightning in the distance, perhaps to avoid looking at me.

"Yeah, right," I responded sarcastically.

"Don't, Shiniwa! You must learn to respect the respected!" When he lowered his head, I was sure he was doing it to avoid showing his great disappointment in me.

But Kako was right. I could not find myself in this simple life as peaceful as it was, lying between two serenely snow-capped mountains. In seven or eight years (time is illusive in such a setting) my journey had taken me from the lap of luxury, to the almost happy life in London, to exile in a place that time and man have both forgotten. Though Kako had been successful in channeling my energies and calming me somewhat, I was still more Michael than Shiniwa. I still boiled inside and resented this quiet place where only men lived who wore strange clothes and softly called each other "GeGe" as they went about their monotonous daily routines. I had to play the rebel, to be the odd man out who was always up to something. I had to let them know. I was the angel they did not pray for, the nightmare they never wanted to dream, the days in a numberless calendar, the prickly cactus in the middle of an ocean.

My only prayer was almost a rail against God, "Angels, touch my soul where I live in this place between nameless mountains, made arid by the sins I am not guilty of and the lies that shell my soul. I'm only a kid!" The answer to my prayer, I know now, was Kako. My friend, my mentor, my punching bag who never gave up on me.

CHAPTER THIRTEEN

DON'T SIT UNDER THE APPLE TREE

WE WERE UNDER THE APPLE TREE AGAIN, KAKO SITTING
with his head against its firm trunk, me standing, straining, resisting
I knew not what. "I am a bird!" I announced, "I wish I could fly. I
would fly so high no one could see me up there!"

"Is it important to be invisible to people if you could fly?" Kako
asked.

"Yes!"

"Why?"

"Because people are jealous like the kids here who cannot play
soccer," I declared.

"Are you jealous of the birds because they can fly and you
cannot?" Kako asked.

"No."

"Why?"

"Because they're not people. They're birds and birds are supposed
to fly!"

I changed the subject and began dancing around, "I'm a dancer!
Look, Kako, see how I dance. I dance to any music . . . (I became
still) . . . except there is no music here." I climbed the apple tree. I
looked down. Kako was agitated like a mother hen that hatched a

brood of ducklings that went for a swim when she led them by a stream.

"Shiniwa, come down. Please, Shiniwa, climb down!" Kako said urgently.

I didn't hear his pleas. Instead I threw myself off the tree limb, my arms spread wide. I felt myself thinking, "Stop me now, world, I am the bird, I'm invisible, you jealous world!"

For a long time I was in pain from a broken leg, a broken arm, a badly bruised and swollen forehead; but most of all from my wounded pride. Kako came and gently rubbed my feet as he prayed softly. I knew it was him, even with my eyes closed I could smell his presence as far as a mile away.

"Shiniwa," Kako said, "Life is given. You cannot refuse it. You may deny life, but it will never refuse you."

"What are you talking about?" I growled, "I fell out of the damn tree!"

Why did I bother to tell lies to Kako? I knew that he knew I was lying. It was almost infuriating that I could never lie to him. I didn't want to be there. I wanted to be with my sister, my grandmother, and Hailie. I didn't even like my ball anymore.

I never told Kako how much he meant to me, that he had literally saved my life. Though I never expressed it to him in words, he was my only family, all I had in that strange and stranded world. I would have jumped off that apple tree again and again, refusing life, had it not been for him.

Dig through my heart that I hold naked in my hands.

For a long time I did not play soccer and the monks would not touch my handmade ball. The pall of silence fell once again over the monastery, and in my depression I opted for the monk's habit—I refused to speak. I was resigned to the silent world as my home from which I could never escape.

Kako was never out of my sight, ever vigilant over my safety and comfort, singing in his beautiful voice to soothe my troubled soul.

My child, who came through the sun
My son, who rose the light
The light of my life
The life of the sun
My son, the burning Shiniwa

He never stopped talking. He told me stories and read to me from books in the monastery library. No convalescent ever had such an attentive nurse.

One day as I was staring into an aimless horizon, I heard a loud whistle. "I made this for you!" Kako said showing me a whistle carved out of a bamboo stick. "I want you to coach the boys again. Can you?" he asked.

I took the whistle and came back to life. Sitting in my director's chair on the sidelines, I yelled at the monks, instructing them on the fine art of playing soccer. I blew the whistle as loud as I could and brought back the pandemonium I had always created among those quiet and peaceful monks. Maybe they had my body isolated in this vacant world, but I had my spirit they could never own. I would enjoy disrupting their dull lives in a protest that said clearly that I didn't want to be there, so my game was their payback for keeping me. The once quiet monastery now sounded like a racetrack because Shiniwa had landed. Kako, my support, always stood beside me, smiling in spite of the chaos that followed me like a tidal wave.

Who knows—in a land where there are no calendars other than the relentless orbit of the sun and the tailgating moon—exactly how many years it took before I finally calmed my tormented soul. It was so gradual that even I was not fully aware of the metamorphosis. I was still wild and obnoxious, but I had learned to control my violent kicking temper; and I threw myself into learning the Monk's language and teaching the younger boys all I could about the English language, which I continued to use even though I was beginning to understand theirs.

A person may change his behavior, but reputations tend to linger, a fact I learned one day when I heard a voice say, "Can I be your friend?"

I looked around at a fat-boy-kid monk who had tasted the impact of my right foot many, many times in the past. He was much larger than I was, but he humbled himself before me in a way I never expected.

"I don't want you to hurt me," he said plaintively, "I have a bad back. It hurts me and I can't sit right. I even have a stomachache and my toe is swollen. Do you think I can be your friend? Do you think I'm dying? Please don't be mad at me. I can help you with your chores."

It was amazing. He stood there like a deer in the headlights waiting for my reaction. My first thought was unkind. I could maybe cut some of that fat off, I mused, but then thought, No, Kako would never allow that. I just looked at him for a long time as he waited nervously for my verdict. I liked his face, and I kind of liked him. It would be nice to have someone to play football with. I was getting bored playing so much by myself.

My answer was non-committal, however, as I ordered, "Come back later!"

He jumped up saying with a big smile, "Oh, yes, Shiniwa," as though he were responding to the voice of God. Quickly he disappeared. His name was Erzifo, the Son of Buddha.

Erzifo became my servant, my player, my comrade, and my punching bag. He never complained and never showed pain. He obeyed without question and served without pay. He was, in fact, my best friend after Kako who was so happy about our friendship that he could not stop bragging about us to the other monks.

I made it a common joke in the monastery that going to bed was to meet and dream of the ice angels. We were the only known polar bears over those frigid mountains that even sun was hesitant to warm. There were icicles hanging by the side of the walls almost every night.

The monastery had very little to offer once the road froze and access to the area around it became impassable. Ice was so thick and the snow depths were unbelievably deep.

The ice glaciers surrounded us and any foolish attempts to create a passage beyond it was suicide. The land knew of only a pristine white snow color.

I held command of a land,
So righteous all I knew
Indeed, I fished an angler in a sand ocean

I always remembered the time Hailie and I sat on that frozen soccer grass when I kissed her. I had told that story to Erzifo a hundred times, but he always wanted me to repeat it. It was as if we lived and shared that memory anytime the cold nights felt like razor sharp needles that nothing could stop it. Erzifo always bombarded me with so many questions about my time in England.

I was hesitant to share my past with anyone except Kako. However, I felt very close to my fat beautiful friend as time went by.

There was a certain kind of naughtiness between us. We were teenagers growing up under strict monastery celibacy rules and talks about females were forbidden. Buddhism takes a strong ethical stand in human affairs and sexual behavior in particular. However, unlike most otherworld religions, most variations of Buddhism do not go into details what is right and what is wrong in mundane activities. The monastery treated that subject as non—existent. The closest things to describe a woman in that monastery were pictures of some ancient queens or baronesses in our limited library books.

I drew and shared a picture of a girl with her boobs sticking out by what I could remember from a commercial I had seen on the television back in England. Erzifo did not know why the girl had bigger breast and I could not explain that to him. We were certainly not asking Kako about that subject. That was our private secret. We would die laughing anytime we could see the ox's big breasts.

Erzifo hid the girl's picture inside his bamboo mattress. I used to kid him about the girl coming to life and asking him to touch her boobs. He used to get scared quite easily.

I made a scarecrow once. I put two cones on her body representing woman's boobs. I used to chase Erzifo all over the monastery with it. The poor soul would scream running away as if a ghost was chasing him.

I took refuge one entire morning in the storage shack when I had a dream of kissing and touching Hailie the night before and wet my robe. I was so embarrassed I took a silence vow for a week. Kako treated that subject with most poise and humor once I broke my silence. I felt he was quite taken back but after all, he was the greatest teacher.

Erzifo played flute he had made from bamboo because I liked it, and he played for me because I was his friend. We spent almost every day together after Kako's daily walks and instruction. Life was easier and everybody in the monastery seemed to breathe a sigh of relief. The devil was gone, just an old man and his two students—Shiniwa and Erzifo. The three of us had another thing in common—each of us had been abandoned to the monastery by our fathers. Erzifo's father left him at the monastery when he was three, promising to return. He never did. The monks took him under their wings and raised him even though nobody really knew how to take care of a small child. They had done the same for me with no experience in caring for an older child with the temper of a Tasmanian devil.

In spite of the camaraderie I now enjoyed, the ember within would flare into flames at unexpected times, and the one person I could never forgive, the events I could never forget threw me into fits of rage. "He cut my sister's right arm. That was her writing arm. He is just a cruel bastard. He used to hit my mother. Do you know how many times my mother has gone to the emergency room to be stitched up? He hit me all the time. The bastard was always drunk. He . . . he . . . (mere words failed to penetrate my rage). That's why I hate him."

Kako would look distressed at my outbursts. It had been a long time since we even touched on that subject, I suppose because Kako hoped I had mellowed and changed my feelings toward my father.

"I wish you had tried to get to know your father better," Kako said.

"I'd do much better never having known him at all!" I responded.

It would pass and Kako would keep on trying. He never gave up on me. He never considered sending me back to the hell I had come from. He was determined to calm my troubled soul. Kako believed in my integrity which he nourished through his teachings he was sure one day would blind me with the light of their truths.

The exchange between master and student never ceased the whole time I was under Kako's tutelage. My most innocuous question usually turned into some kind of lesson I was supposed to learn.

"What's on the other side of these mountains?" I asked Kako one day.

"I will take you there one day."

"You've never been outside of this area. Have you?" I asked.

"Yes. I have," Kako said.

"Why don't you go there more often?" I questioned.

"I have what I need here!" he said.

"You have nothing. What are you talking about?" I replied angrily.

"Name one thing I need that I do not have here," he smiled

"Life man, you need a life!" I said defiantly.

"Life is given," he said pointing to the sky.

"A life of what?" I asked, ridiculing him

"The only real failure in life is not to be true to the best one knows. No one saves us but ourselves. No one can and no one may. We ourselves must walk the path," Kako said.

I recall waking up and finding Kako sitting on the edge of my bamboo mat, smiling down at me. "What are you doing?" I demanded.

"I couldn't resist the temptation of observing you laugh out loud in your sleep," he said, laughing loudly himself. I realized that he was sharing my laughter. A kind of poem came into my mind, "Share my dreams my aged friend, my dreams of black and white."

"Can we go fishing in the lake?" I asked Kako one morning, "There are bunches of fish in it. I have seen them myself."

"Yes, we can. But on my terms only," Kako responded.

We walked up the mountain and descended to the lake on the opposite side. It was a beautiful and pristine lake with many colorful wild flowers all around. There were millions of butterflies that created waves of elegant colors as they flitted around. The always noisy monkeys were bathing in the lake, but there were not many birds that I could see.

"Welcome to Shahla's Lake!" Kako announced. I thought it was the most beautiful poem I had ever heard, this most pristine lake named for the angel herself. But we had come here to fish, so I looked at Kako to find out if he had any fishing gear. He did not.

"How do you expect me to catch the fish?" I asked.

"Watch the monkeys," he said.

"You think I am a monkey? I can't catch those sleazy fish with my bare hands," I protested.

"Shiniwa, observe the monkeys. Look at their legs. How they bend. How they look at the fish and use their hands to scoop up the fish. Remember, I did say we would come fishing under my terms," Kako said.

All right then! I jumped into the cold waters of the lake filled by the streams of melting snow. It was so frigid that I could not breathe. I started sinking to the bottom fast, struggling to swim back to the top. It was then that I saw a huge fish with the strangest face . . . my father's! He opened his jaws to swallow me and I was so horrified, I froze. I could not move a muscle, paralyzed, sinking.

I came to hearing Kako's voice, "You poor child, Shiniwa! You scared me to death. Why did you do that? You don't know how to swim." I felt Kako's hands pushing against my chest.

I caught no fish that day; what I caught was a dreadful cold that made me delirious with fever and chills. Kako never left the foot of my straw mat as the entire manpower of the monastery came and went, being of service to the little Knight of the Thames, Sir Shiniwa, the one boy wrecking crew who had indelibly left his mark on the place as well as on the bodies of those who felt his rage. In my hallucinations, I was mounted on the back of a strutting Dookie roaming the countryside like Don Quixote between the two snow-capped mountains. Sir Knight-With-No-Name in a place with no name, an orphan imprisoned and exiled even from any dreams of the big city with double-decker buses. In my burning fever I slid down the sharp edge of my nightmare, visiting places of great horror and meeting people I never knew. Judge me as a boy riding his red crowned rooster for the crimes you accuse me of! Why are you so cruel? Life, march on! How long I was so ill is hard to say in that place with no calendar, where time never matters.

"Okay, girls, keep your heads up and stop throwing your arms around like it is a boxing match," I was yelling at the boys of the monastery playing on the world's funniest soccer field. I was back again after my long illness.

There was something always wrong when the boys were running after the ball. Their robes would wrap around their legs and they would fall down, getting bruised all over. I stopped the game and lined them up, walking up to them as though I were some army sergeant doing a routine inspection. I rolled their robes up, knotting them around their waists. They looked like a bunch of pregnant women. Their legs were freer to run but they looked really funny.

It took a lot of effort to convince the master to allow us to wear our designer robe jerseys. I actually persuaded the monk who was in charge of the robes to tailor new ones, cut short like soccer trunks with a semi tank top jersey. I succeeded in establishing the first ever monks soccer team unknown to the world, the world that did not exist.

Team Shiniwa wins Himalayan Soccer cup—BBC Sports headline that never was

Our master Ouiyen, whose name was Kyi, meaning clear, and spoke slowly and softly that sometimes felt like perpetuity. Nobody dared to say or do anything when he spoke. He talked succinctly and always to the point. His words were very positive and poised. He always admired and esteemed everybody around calling them by their first names.

I always thought he was strange. He spoke looking directly into your face with biggest black eyes that never lost directions.

He only spoke when we all had massed around the kitchen. There were times he did not speak a single word for a month.

I could see his lips moving very gently and slowly but never hearing anything.

Master Kyi was a short man with an unbelievable built body. He walked gracefully and firm.

"I am the music you don't hear. I am the light, dark you shall see".

Master Kyi was in one of those silence vows when I gave him a visit one mid—afternoon.

It was a beautiful early spring day. It was not surprising cold for the time of the year rather very pleasant. Snow was everywhere. You could hear the rush of the wild life all around us. We were all finishing our daily churns and getting ready to assemble in the soccer field for an afternoon game.

The game was the daily event that no one would miss.

The monks, who would not talk, could most definitely play.

Shiniwa had changed the rules.

"Master Ouiyen". I called upon Master Kyi

He was praying and moving his head around very gently. He lowered his beads pointing me to sit.

I sat right across from him next to small altar with many small cups and scents.

It was a common practice to sit behind him to the right, but not for Shiniwa. I followed no such culture.

I saw him smile as he reached through the altar. He looked at my hand. I offered him my open fist. He put a small white marble in the palm of my hand.

He lowered his head dipping back into his own cogitation world. I waited a few minutes to see if he would say something. The world in that monastery was so small and dreadfully quiet. I was getting ready to leave when I remembered I had gone to see him for a reason. We were short of players. Six of the monks had left the previous day to collect wood from the forest, which was normally a couple of days trip from the monastery.

"Master Ouiyen". I said again.

"We do not have enough players today. I am here to recruit you. You can play any position you like". I insisted.

Master Ouiyen raised his head looking directly into my eyes. His face looked so beautiful and saintly. His eyes were so shiny with a strange glorious glare. He looked at me for a long time and suddenly burst into laughter I still hear it to this day. The laughter was so loud and so unexpected that I actually jumped back to the corner of the room.

I thought he had gone crazy.

He did not stop laughing. I did not know what to do. I had never heard him talking loudly. He was laughing uncontrollably.

He was a man of great integrity and utmost respect. That afternoon he was acting like a happy child going to circus.

"When the sun sets it shines gloriously the dark you never see".

I never understood what really happened in that spring afternoon. All I remember that I rushed out of master's quarter not looking back hearing his laughter all the way to the soccer field.

CHAPTER FOURTEEN

THE GOLDEN MONKEY

NORMAL LIFE IN THE MONASTERY WAS QUITE SIMPLE but lack of materials had made it quite challenging. We never had enough fire logs to burn so heat was very limited and the place was always very cold. We were always hungry but no one ever complained. We all had different errands and labors to do. However, we worked as a team with no expectations or any need to ask for help. There was something to be done and it would be done. I worked in the kitchen cutting the vegetables. We grew those vegetables inside the monastery because of the cold outside temperatures. I tended a little rice patty we had at the bottom of the valley. It was a rough and back breaking constant labor, but it was the only source of rice we had.

There was a small indoor storage where we kept our supplies. It was almost impossible to find any other sources of food during winter months. However, we were not alone. The golden monkeys were constantly badgering us and stealing food even though we were trying to keep them away and keep our supplies locked up. I was quite disturbed by the fact that we had to fight constantly with the monkeys over the food, though the monks were relaxed and content.

Every time I charged at the monkeys, Kako would ask me to respect them and not to scream at them. One day while I was in the kitchen, I forgot to keep the kitchen door closed. I was busy chopping and preparing the vegetables when I heard a noise behind me. Turning to see what the noise was, I saw one of those nasty thieving golden monkeys trying to pull open the rice bag. I yelled at him and he hissed back.

I don't know what happened but I found myself kicking the monkey in the head as hard as I could. The poor monkey flew halfway across the kitchen and landed by the wall motionless. I walked to him. He was dead with his neck twisted and his eyes staring right at me as if asking me why. I froze. I did not know what to do. I sat by the monkey's body but did not dare to touch it. It was a horrible feeling. I felt so guilty and so cruel. I just sobbed.

I managed to get out and walk to Kako who was deep in prayer. I tapped him on his shoulder. He looked at me, so I just kneeled next to him speechless.

I was a murderer and a cruel savage. Kako sensed my distress and held me in his arms touching my head.

"Shiniwa, what is wrong?"

I pointed to the kitchen.

Kako rushed to the kitchen while I sat outside and waited. It was like eternity before he merged out of the kitchen. He was holding the dead body of the monkey in his arms. He stood by me as he put the dead body of the monkey by my feet.

"Did you do this?"

I only sobbed and he knew his answer.

"Get up. Get up now!" Kako yelled at me, "Pick him up! Pick him up and follow me!"

He had never yelled at me before, but he was yelling now and very upset.

Trembling, I picked up the monkey's lifeless body and followed him. We walked outside of the monastery where he climbed a small hill toward the lush forest.

There he stood by the tallest tree where he and I used to sit as he talked about everything he could think of.

"Put the monkey down and start digging!" Kako ordered.

I had no choice except to obey. I knew how to make a shovel from the bamboo sticks, and that's what I did. It felt miserable as I was digging with Kako standing there wordless and motionless. I dug a big hole and moved to put the monkey's body in it.

"No, dig more!" He ordered.

I dug more, so deep I would need him to pull me out. I was very tired and thirsty, but I kept on digging. It was getting late and I was truly exhausted; but Kako just stood there motionless while I continued to dig. I looked at him to receive his approval but he only stood there without any gestures or words.

"Can I come out? Is it deep enough?" I asked.

"Keep digging, I will let you know!" Kako said.

I wondered how much deeper, but I knew I had no choice.

I had dug so deep that I was unable to throw the dirt out, but I just kept on digging.

"I'm hungry. Can we go back and get something to eat? Plus it's dark now and I can't see anything," I said.

"Keep on digging and if you are tired you may rest inside there and if hungry you may eat the dirt. After all, it's what this monkey will have once we put him down there in that hole," Kako said.

I was getting scared. It was not like Kako. I had never seen Kako so angry. I could have easily walked away but I had too much respect for him to defy him. I lay against the dirt wall inside the giant hole I had dug. The next I knew, I could feel the sun's warmth on my face.

I had fallen asleep inside the monkey's grave. I looked up. Kako was sitting by the edge of the hole, motionless.

"Keep on digging!" He said.

My whole body was aching but I resumed digging. I became outraged as hours went by. It was getting really hot inside the hole. I was fatigued and starving. I had a hard time digging as my man made bamboo shovel was completely worn away. At that moment, Kako threw another shovel down the hole without a word.

By midday, I ran out of energy. I was so fatigued I had no more strength to even stand inside the hole. I was completely shattered. I was so humiliated.

I knew why he was doing this to me. He was not punishing me. He wanted me to feel the death I had caused of another living being. He wanted to show how useless I was at the bottom of the hole I had dug. He wanted me to feel the pain I had caused. I sat there.

Sometime later, something landed next to me. It was a piece of bread and a small jar of water. I swallowed the bread and drank the water. I knew if Kako wanted me to get out of that hole he would have said so. There was a deadly silence. I picked up the shovel and continued digging. I had no coordination. My hands and feet were swollen and numb. I was dizzy and disoriented. I fell down unconscious. When I came to myself, I could see the stars above the hole. I was cold. I started to climb up the hole when a big pile of dirt let go and I fell back to the bottom.

"Kako, Kako!" I screamed. "Kako are you there? Can you help me up?"

I begged, exhausted and shivering.

"You will come out when I say so. Dig!" I heard Kako's voice out of the darkness.

I could not believe it. I was stuck inside my own grave. I was getting mad but I tried to control myself. It had taken all these years to calm my nerves down and learn to use my hands to construct rather than to destroy. I thought about Erzifo, about my sister and my grandmother. I had not thought about them for a long time.

I thought about the time I was stuck between the chair legs while I was trying to crawl through the classroom while Mrs. Foresstes was writing on the chalkboard. It was so embarrassing. My neck was stuck and I could not free myself. I was marched to the principal's office with the chair on my head, Mrs. Foresstes Sheppard me while the entire class snickered in mocking laughter.

"Well, well!" the principal smiled, rather gladly to see me in that awkward position. "Maybe we should leave him in there for a while. He looks cute like that!" he said.

Déjà vous. I knew I didn't look cute inside that hole, rather miserable and in a lot of pain.

There was a story about a man who was being hung. He started to cry just before execution. The executioner stopped and asked why he was crying. The man said because he was embarrassed to go without paying for his crimes. I was just a thirteen year old kid whose only crime was to be there. I had come to accept my verdict.

I was not going anywhere. I slept another night in that hole. I was so hungry I ate dirt and started to throw up.

Before the sun came up the next morning, I was awake and waiting.

"You may come up!" Kako said.

I had no strength to climb up out of that hole but I tried. Then I felt Kako's hand lifting me. Once out of the deep hole, I looked around to find the monkey's body, but it was not there.

"Where is the monkey?" I asked.

"Start filling up the hole. Then you can go back!" Kako said.

I never found out where the monkey went.

> *Life has no surprises, it is merely*
> *what it is. How we treat the*
> *lessons learned from great*
> *teaching is what surprises us.*

CHAPTER FIFTEEN

ERZIFO

IT WAS A LOVELY SUMMER EVENING. SUMMER NIGHTS were normally breezy but quite pleasant. The dazzling sky was showing off the galaxies of unblemished stars veiled to the polluted outside world.

The monastery was surrounded by the harshest rudiments of nature, but nights were different. The elevated platform where the monastery was situated along with clear, cool nights presented a gift of cherubic surprises with pallid sky and shooting stars. The nights felt like living within the Milky Way in your bedroom.

You had to dodge the meteors and stars looking so close you could see through them to warm your frozen hands.

The outlying forest twisted deafening noises. The golden monkeys persuasive piercing screams allured each other to join the feast all night long.

The wild boars were akin to doomed militia marching within the profuse forest trees playing the marching band.

The while owls would hoot anytime there was a break between all those shattering noises.

The forest at night performed powerful sound track of some Italian Opera Singer and a carnival of lights for the wing-lit butterflies. The light waves of butterflies were like fanning thousands of flashlights in all directions. The nights were full of mysteries and unanswered questions.

The nights were also Erzifo and I favorite times to sit by the rock formations by the cliffs overlooking an endless horizon with our feet dangling freely in the open space.

I never remember my mother. Do you remember your mother? Erzifo asked.

Yes! I responded nonchalantly.

Ouiyen once said that my father dumped me here promising to return but he never did. Do you remember your father? Erzifo asked again

Yes. I looked at him angrily.

Do you know where they are? Are they alive? He asked in the most innocent way.

Yes! I clinched my fist trying hard to control my resentment toward his questions.

I remembered Kako's teachings: "Anger will prison your soul. Reason with your heart and answer later".

So, why are you here?

Erzifo was really pissing me off. He had never interrogated me like that before. He was normally very non-challenging and quiet. I expected him to play his flute and let the night fly. He was on a mission that night.

Why are you asking me all these questions? I asked with an intimidating tone.

I love you and want to know more about you. You are like a mystery. You are all I have here. Master Kako is Ouiyen but you are better than anything else I have ever known. I want to know if I can carry some of your pains. I want to wear your wounds. I will sell my soul to devil for you. I will do anything for you. Erzifo eyes were like SHOG River and his voice trembling.

Erzifo's remarks were heart breaking.

I felt very weak. I sat quietly. I felt my own tears. I turned my head not to let Erzifo see my tears.

I wanted to tell him that I was not a mystery rather a weak stranded little boy who was banned to have a normal life and abandoned to perish. I was an orphan with many parents. Although I owned everything, fate kept them in a locked gold vault and the key thrown to the bottom of the sea.

I remembered my big home in the richest tiers and the opulent surroundings. I flew through the marble floors of our house. I saw my grandmother knotting a black shawl. Shahla was sitting by her desk writing in her favorite poem notebook. Dookie was happily roaming around. I saw my father's room. I tried to close my eyes at no avail. He was sitting there with his bottle at his side. I was grinding my teeth with rage.

"Your grandmother's dead. Just like your sister". My father shouted at me spitting.

I looked back to where I had seen my grandmother. She was not there. Nobody was there.

I was horrified. I felt a deep chill. I heard my father's satanic laughs.

"Grandma, grandma". I screamed as hard I could.

Shiniwa, Shiniwa. I heard my name. Somebody was shacking me violently.

Erzifo was holding my hands and pulling me. His face looked so frightened covered with tears.

I sat straight and tried to hold my composure together. My whole body was shaking uncontrollably and my face was sweating profusely.

Erzifo put his hands around my shoulder holding me as hard as he could, crying.

I felt broken. Shiniwa's sun had set one more time. Shiniwa's galaxy was starless.

That night, Erzifo played his flute softly as tears felt through our eyes, his hand on my shoulder and our feet dangling in suspense.

Dreams
Stronger than a worrier soul
Mad as a volcano
Higher than any sun
Colder than ice
Wild as the ocean waves
The rivers' rage
But, yet
So small, housed in a boy's heart

Erzifo never again questioned me about my past.
I never told my friend about my family.
I never told him how I missed my grandmother.
He did not learn that my sister was in heavens.
He never met my father.

CHAPTER SIXTEEN

SECRET

KAKO AND I WERE WALKING PAST THE OLD MAN Mdogho farm who was running around and yelling at his mule. I always felt bad about how terribly I expressed my unsought judgment on the old man. I waved at him bowing. The old Mdogho yelled at the mule who stopped immediately. He started walking toward where we were. I knew we were not suppose to talk to the villagers. I was not so sure what to do. I looked at Kako who had a grim on his face watching the old man approaching us.

"Hello Master Kako. This young man should be Shiniwa. I am very happy to see you". The old man Mdogho said.

I had no idea what was going on and how the old man knew about me. I thought we were not allowed to talk to the villagers. I looked at Kako suspiciously.

Kako bowed at the old man holding his hands. The old man Mdogho hugged Kako tightly. That seemed quite eccentric but I kept my mouth shut. The old man put his hands on my shoulders and said something that I could not understand.

The two men talked a while before the old jovial man approached me again.

"Come to my place for some fish. Come tomorrow". He said.

I didn't know what to say. I wasn't very sure if I could even talk to him.

Kako came to my rescue. You can talk, can't you?

Of course. But, what was that mambo jumbo about not talking to the villagers? I was quite agitated. How does he know my name? could you explain to me what is going on? I am really confused.

Kako smiled. He said something to Mdogho that I did not understand. The old man Mdogho started walking back to his ramshackle place when Kako pointed me to sit next to him on the side of the dirt footpath.

Chinese have occupied the land not far from here. They have killed and imprisoned thousands of innocent people. Although, our monastery is not within their grasp, their soldiers have in the past crossed the border in the hunt of anybody protesting against their occupation. Master Quiyen has asked us to be very cautious about some newcomers to this area. They are Han Chinese who constantly cross the border to come here. They use their money and their government backing to infiltrate within these very simple villagers. They have hired some of the locals as their spies. A few villagers have disappeared. At one point, some villagers had taken refuge inside the monastery that jeopardized the existence of us all. Master Ouiyen had instructed us to follow the non-combative approach toward the conflicts to maintain peace. Mdogho has been the mediator between the monastery and the villagers for many years. He is also a very good friend to me. I told him about you when he asked. However, his knowledge about you is very limited to your name and that you are my own son". Kako said.

I like to accept his invitation to lunch. He knows we don't eat fish. Why is he offering fish to me for lunch? I asked precariously.

He was just testing you. Kako seemed very proud of me.

Can I take Erzifo with me? I asked. I knew Erzifo would have loved to feast on some more food as the allotment at the monastery was never enough.

I think Erzifo would love the idea. Kako said pointedly.

We sat there for a short period before Mdogho came back with some fruits and a bowl of water. He offered them to us quite humbly. We drank the water and store the fruit in Kako's little backpack.

"Tomorrow lunch". Mdogho yelled as we started going back to the monastery, I forgot to ask him if it was ok to take Erzifo with me. I exclaimed.

It's ok. He knows. Kako said.

The next day when Erzifo and I arrived at the old man Mdogho place, I saw him standing by his little shack waiting for us. He seemed to be very cheerful and in good spirit. He hugged us taking us inside his place. His one room hut looked clean with various life necessities and some very old pictures. There was food at the corner of the room on top of a small table. He invited us to sit and dine with him. That was the kind of invitation Erzifo would never refuse. I noticed a very old picture of a young soldier standing in attention. I asked the old man Mdogho about the young soldier. He opened a small wooden chest taking a worn out helmet that looked exactly the same as the one in the picture. He put it on smiling very proudly. He told us he was a soldier in the World War II and he fought the enemies that he never identified.

The old man Mdogho seemed a lot more zealous than I had given him credit for. He picked up an old wooden instrument and started playing. It made the most soothing sound I had ever heard. I could see his only good eye staring through the small tattered window. I was lost in my sweetest dreams through his music. Something that I had not heard in a very long time. We sat at his door step afloat a galaxy so different from the one within those devious lofty walls. The old man mollified us forgetting who we were. We spent the whole day with the old man whose gracious hospitality were inconceivable.

We were getting ready to leave when Mdogho handed us two straw hats as a token of his appreciation.

"Come here tomorrow. I want to show you a secret". The old man Mdogho said.

We thanked him and agreed to return if Kako would have permitted that. After all, who would reject the idea of finding a secret in a place as boring as that hell land.

On our return trip, Erzifo could not stop talking about the old man. His excitement was overwhelming. I was glad to think of him when I received the invitation from the old Mdogho.

Kako was very happy to listen to our day's story. He seemed he had found a new source to heal my wounds and did not hesitate to let us return the next day after the prayer mountain.

Erzifo was so animated he could not sleep that night. I felt asleep whilst Erzifo was asking so many questions that I had no answers to them.

Erzifo woke me up way before everybody else to go to prayer mountain. Kako was waiting for us at the monstrous gate once we climbed down the prayer mountain. He handed us some food instructing us to be respectful and courteous to the old man. He refused answering my question about Mdogho secret.

Mdogho met us at the edge of his farm with a small package on his back. He asked us to follow him through the thick forest on a path that was quite unfamiliar to me. He was extremely potent for an old man. He was walking so swift we had to almost run to catch up with him.

The forest was getting so intense that the old man had to machete our way through the twigs. The jungle sounds and the indescribable trees' canopies dampened the hard work of cutting our way through the foliages. The trekking was no challenge for our phenomenal physical shapes. However, we had to struggle pushing our bodies through some heavily bounded shrubberies.

I was wondering what kind of secret would have required such a physical exertion. Erzifo had curious perplexed stares.

After a few hours, we arrived at what looked like an underground tunnel. It was blocked by bushes secured by tree logs. It did not take us long to move some of the logs to create an opening. Once inside, Mdogho lit a couple of candles. There was standing knee high water inside, but it didn't smell bad. It felt like a small spring flow. I didn't know what to assume but I was getting more and more excited. Erzifo was breathless.

Once we traveled through the tunnel, we emerged from an area which was hard to envisage. It was a large open area with very tall trees surrounding it. There were chocolate box vibrant flower fields all around. We started walking toward the flower fields. The surface felt hard with many cracks. I stopped to examine the surface of what turned to look like hard old asphalt completely covered with flowers emergent through the cracks. There were a few completely hidden tarnished wooden structures against the wild overgrown vegetations. The buildings looked ghosted. We started to run toward the shells.

Mdogho waved us to stop. He asked us to just follow him and not touch or move anything. I remembered Kako's orders to fully respect the old man.

The old Mdogho pushed to open what seemed like a gate to the biggest building. It was quite rusted and hard to open. The gate frame would not let ajar. Mdogho used a long metal shaft that laid to the side of the gate to force it wide enough for us to get in.

Once inside, Erzifo and I stopped on our tracks. It was a much larger building than it seemed from outside. It didn't have high ceiling but it was quite deep. There were mechanical tools, tires, benches, barrels, small container tanks, chains and a lot more. I tried to fathom at what I was looking at.

Erzifo was speechless. The old man Mdogho had a big smile on his face.

"Let me show you the secret". The old man Mdogho exclaimed merrily trying to show off his riches.

He cracked a small side gate to the adjacent building. We almost broke each others knees trying to get through.

I was unable to comprehend what I was looking at. There were two very old airplanes parked side by side in the second building.

Erzifo kneed praying. He had no idea what they were. His face was filled with joy and fear. I wasn't very sure how I felt. I had not seen any of these western toys for many years. Erzifo had never seen an airplane before. It was like a dream.

We walked closer to the planes. They looked identical with different paintings under their nose. One of them had faded yellow single tooth painting as if to bite anybody getting too close. The other had a small almost green color band around its nose. The propellers were still intact with many cracks and dents showing the storage age. There were faint Red Circles painted in the middle of their fuselages. There were numbers on their tails with glass canopies. I remembered Mrs. Foresstes class talking about Japanese fighters and Kamikazes. Was I looking at a Zero Japanese Fighter in a land where time had forgotten?

Erzifo was all over me quizzical about those strange bits and pieces. He was so scared and so curious that didn't know what to do with himself. I needed some elucidation myself. It was way too convoluted to explain to a boy who grew up in a monastery all his life.

Mdogho looked like a little boy showing off his many marbles. He climbed into the cockpit of one of the planes wearing a leather helmet. I followed him up the plane standing outside of the glass cockpit canopy tattooed with cow-webs. The cockpit looked surprising clean. I had seen picture of cockpits but this was quite different from whatsoever I had seen before. All the instrumentations were different. There were many loose wires and the stick was out of place.

I had a bag of questions to ask but, I was enjoying myself so much that I decided not to spoil the moment with interrogating the old man.

Erzifo's fear had left him crippled by the plane's nose gear. I put my hands around the cockpit canopy and laid my head against its cold surface. I tried to pilot that plane through my own ingenious horizon. I don't remember how long I had been there when I heard the old man Mdogho asking me to let go and climb down.

Mdogho invited us to sit under the wing of the plane. He offered us some food from his small package he had carried all morning. His eyes were wedged to the planes. Erzifo looked so funny and amused. His mouth was wide open. He was completely consumed in his little world that owed him so much.

I tried to explain to Erzifo what an airplane was. I told him that they were like metallic birds carrying human to the air. I could not explain why and how those flying machines killed people. I didn't know how to describe the actions of Japanese kamikazes as I remember very little. I knew I has seen some old books at the monastery that could have helped immensely.

The old man Mdogho knew about that place for over twenty years. During World war II, this was a small Japanese air base supporting their Indo-China operations in that part of the world. However, somehow during the last days of the war, Japanese had temporarily abandoned that base hoping to return. Mdogho who was a soldier had killed the only two Japanese Guards in the base, burring their bodies not far from that small hangar. Mdogho who had traveled to investigate some strange noises deep from inside the forest, had discovered the base. The Japanese Guards had opened fire and Mdogho managed to kill both of them in gun battle. His guilty conscious had forced him to keep that place a clandestine.

We roamed around the dilapidated air base all afternoon before heading back to beat the darkness of the jungle.

There was a deadly silence walking back. I was trying to picture the gun battle. It was hard to think of that desolate place which served as an enigmatic hidden air base that almost certainly killed many innocent people. I tried to re-live the lives of those who once occupied that place. I imagined taking off in those planes zooming through the dense forest. I didn't hear the jungle clamor anymore but I could hear those Japanese pilots ordering their crews around. I re-staged Mrs. Foresstes class conversation about Pearl Harbor. I was always enthralled with those flying marvels. My uncle was an air force general and pilot. I remembered my mother took us to his air show as special guests. I had never forgotten that moment when a F-4 Phantom pilot lifted me into his cockpit.

The old man Mdogho life long secret had enthused something very particular in my life.

Hours of travelling to that base seemed like a fast minute back to the monastery. Kako was anxiously waiting for us. Kako did not allow me to talk. He pointed to the glittery moon and said we should talk when moon was latent.

Erzifo and I huddled anxiously in our sleeping quarter. We talked inaudibly all night.

I walked to the lion heads long before crack of dawn. I was surprised to see Kako sitting there. I sat next to him. He put his hand around my shoulders.

He told me he knew of the old man Mdogho's secret. He had persuaded the old man to share that secret with us as a moral lesson that we could not share with anybody. I didn't dare to challenge the issue. I just let go.

Kako never allowed us to return to that air base despite my constant persistence. Erzifo and I talked privately about that day for a long time. I drew a picture of a plane with a Red Circle in the middle of it that Erzifo had tagged above his bed.

CHAPTER SEVENTEEN

HUSTLING FOR BOOKS

KAKO APPEARED VERY HAPPY THE DAY WE SET OUT FOR Luery monastery. He told me, "It has been a while since we last went over there. I am excited to go because they have a lot of books there."

"Where do they get their books from?" I asked.

"There was an old British gentleman who used to travel there very frequently before he passed away, always taking many gifts to that monastery. Luery really enjoyed all those gifts especially the books. We only have very few of them here. You have seen them." Kako could not stop talking, he was so excited.

The next morning, we closed the mighty gates behind us as we walked toward Iuery like an Indian tribe with the ox in the lead. Nobody was left behind. The monks were in a cheerful mood, singing songs that I had never heard before. The whole thing took on the atmosphere of a holy pilgrimage. Only one of the group dressed like a monk was not thinking anything spiritual. I was planning how to get my hands on the books that Luery had. They would not give us those books by just simply asking and violence was out of question; there are ways . . . there are ways.

We arrived there after three days of an excruciating hike. It was totally unlike our ancient guardhouse. Luery was on much lower ground between two valleys, not as green as ours but in a very peaceful area surrounded by a couple of lakes. The building was a much more modern than our battlefield with a lot of colorful statutes and banners.

Luery was a unique monastery and village rolled into one. It was situated amidst breathtaking scenery, the journey to Luery was splendid no matter how you arrived.

The layout of the Luery monastery complex formed a giant Mandela, a representation of the Buddhist universe, and modeled after some Indian temple.

The complex was surrounded by a tall strong wall topped by 1008 (108 is a sacred number) tiny chortens and pierced by gates at the four cardinal points.

The main temple in the center represented some mythical mountain at the center of the Buddhist universe.

There were three large chortens at the corners of the main temple in three different colors, symbolizing Sun.

The main temple was a grand two-story building that occupied the center of the monastery. There were hidden murals on some of the walls. The first floor was the most impressive, and was dominated by the main assembly hall, with old Mandalas on the high ceiling.

Flanking the entrance to the main chapel were statues of figures associated with Samye, Shantarakshita, Padmasambhava, Trisong Detsen and Songtsen Gampo of the respected Buddhist prophesies.

The chapel was accessed through tall doorways and enshrined a statue of Buddha.

There was a small assembly hall in the temple, which housed a beautiful statue of one eye carefully painted on the palm of each of his thousand hands.

There were eerie statues of some Bon demons that were turned into fierce Buddhist protector deities.

The second floor was an open roof area, where monks and locals carried out the craftwork for the temple.

There were barred, glass-fronted case full of wonderful relics laid at the corner of main shrine.

The top floor had an excellent view from the mountains.

The three brightly colored chortens (white, red and green) at the main temple's corners were wooden and each one was slightly different. Inside them were stairs and tiny chapels.

The rest of the buildings were used for different purposes with some being used as stables and others as sleeping quarters.

We were received well. The other monks were much more cheerful than our group even though their place was as quiet as ours.

The next morning, Erzifo and I were kicking the ball around when one of the older monks from Luery approached us wanting to know what we were doing. That was the moment I came up with the idea of how to hustle books from Luery.

It did not take long before I managed to have a scrimmage between my monastery and the Luery monks. I spent an entire morning teaching them the finer points of the game. Before the match started, I briefed my boys to let the Luery players score big and make monkeys out of us. We acted as though we had never played the game that I had taught the Luery monks that morning. Kako and the rest of my monastery's monks were disgusted by the way we played, but the Luery monks were so happy that evening that they baked fresh bread.

We pulled the same scam the next morning, even though there was a lot of resistance from my team, but none of them dared to challenge my authority.

The next morning I found the Luery Ouiyen walking happily along the main entrance. Somehow, I managed to challenge him to let his team play against us for a prize to show our appreciation for their hard work and their hospitality. When the game began, it seemed like an old Roman arena with the Caesar and his Governors looking down at what they expected to be a quick victory. Luery monks could not believe their eyes once the game began. We were in our monk designer jerseys, ready to kill. The poor Luery monks could not even see the fastball with me dribbling it and passing it to Erzifo for the score. During that game, Luery monks had less than five percent possession as we claimed the prize. The next morning, headed back to our monastery, the ox was pulling his wagon with books stacked to the top. Kako never stopped preaching at me for what I had done; however, he was so happy about the books, he decided to postpone my punishment.

The day of reckoning came not only from Kako, but also from the Ouiyen of Luery monastery, where apparently the monks there had been spending a great deal of time discussing the incorrigible boy with the soccer ball. One afternoon, upon my return from the rice paddies, I saw a big donkey by the monastery yard. It was the biggest burro I had ever seen. I approached the beast to pet him and he almost bit me. Returning to my old self, I was about to kick the animal in the face when I heard a voice behind me, "You are a very young warrior and very selfish. I have come here to see you."

Initially, I did not recognize him as it was shadowy dark and he had lowered his head to bow to me. I bowed back to him perfunctorily. When I straightened up, I found it was master Ouiyen from Luery monastery standing there. He had deep big black eyes, which resembled laser lights pointing like a straight edged sword to cut through my face. The eyes were focused and never blinking or ever moving as we walked inside near the kitchen.

"I know you are hungry. I have peeled some oranges for you, take them," he said.

At my monastery, we had a few orange trees that hardly had any oranges and what there were usually got eaten by the birds. A plump, ripe orange at our no-name monastery was a real treat.

I took the peeled orange from him and swallowed part of it just before realizing that all of the monks were listening and watching us. Suddenly, the orange tasted like poison as I realized what I had done. In a place where food was so scarce and we were all always hungry, sharing and caring for each other was the basic principle. I had just failed that test.

I moved to a row of wooden benches made from tree trunks. Their surface was unpolished. I always cut myself sitting on their sharp edges. It was a common practice that we never sat on the same bench twice as every gathering meant sitting next to someone different. We were all the same and nobody had priority—except in deference toward age. My face was burning with shame at having let down Kako with my social gaff in spite of all his instruction.

Then it dawned on me. I had sat while master Ouiyen still standing. In a desperate move and to save whatever bit of face I could, I jumped up to let him have a seat. But he put his hands on my face and gently forced me back down.

"I have been riding on the burro for quite some time. I like to be standing. I like looking at your young face Shiniwa."

I sat quietly, a consummate bundle of misery and shame.

"I have brought you something I know for fact you like," he said walking to the corner of the kitchen. He opened a big wrapped bundle that contained a lot of books.

I could hear the joy throughout the monastery. Everybody expressed their delight by prayers. I felt no joy, however. The books represented the chicanery by which I had gotten others from Iuery. The Ouiyen was showing me that all I needed to do was ask for books, not perform a scam to get them.

He was not finished with me yet as the monks gathered around the books unable to read them because of the diminishing light and our lack of candles at the time. He opened another bag and brought out candles, sharing that precious commodity with us as well. Everything he did was like driving a knife through my wretched heart.

Master Ouiyen was still not done.

"I have something else for you Shiniwa," he said as he pulled a small, colored wooden box neatly decorated with bamboo sticks.

"Open it," he ordered.

I didn't know what to do or say anymore. I was beside myself. I could not believe that he had traveled those difficult miles from Luery to our place just to give me those books and whatever was in this box.

Such misery I felt at that moment. Kako had punished me physically and mentally after what I had done by conning the Luery monks out of a wagonload of books. I had literally stolen those books from them through complete deceit and Kako had never let me forget it in his own way. He had named one of the lion head statutes, which were by the monastery small shrine "Luery".

"Shiniwa, do you think the lion head can hurt you?" Kako asked.

"No," I replied.

"Well, how about taking your things or eating your food?" he asked.

"No," I said again.

"What if you sit on him and get a free ride? What if you throw something at him? How about just beating him with your kicks?" Kako continued questioning.

I was getting quite restless.

"What are you getting at?" I protested.

"I am going to name him Luery. I believe that is a deserving name for him after what you have accomplished back at Luery," Kako said.

From that day, anytime we were passing by the lion head, Kako saluted him calling his given name, "Luery." He occasionally left my food by the lion head asking me to fetch it before leaving for the classroom under the apple tree.

Now, with everyone watching me, I opened the colored box. There was a beautiful white robe inside. I pulled it out admiring it.

"A monk will receive a white robe upon leaving earth. It is a token of his fair dealings and saintly purity. A monk has to wait for that reward," Master Ouiyen said as he walked toward me.

"You are a masterful warrior and a young monk. You are proud and reckless. You are selfish but full of passion. You are a leader but many things you must learn.

I came to thank you and give you this gift. We thought for many days before deciding on this robe. It is for what you brought to us. Your game! Every monk in our monastery looks forward to running after the ball once his daily chores are done. It is part of our daily life along with our martial arts training. We want to beat you next time we have another game with you," Mater Ouiyen said.

I was just frozen and stunned. Here, in an unknown place on no map with no known society, this old astute master had traveled days on a stupid burro to bring me books and his gratitude. It did not fail to register on me that there is a huge disparity between his behavior and the social conventions of the so-called civilized world.

That robe I wore on special occasions. It was both a symbol of honor and my hair shirt to remind me of my humiliation.

CHAPTER EIGHTEEN

XIONE

"Life does not need saving. You redeem your life saving your soul".

The tragedy of life is not that it ends so soon,
but that we wait so long to begin it

IT WAS A COLD WINTER MORNING.

I was sitting by the lion heads when I heard a cracking sound behind me. I looked around to find one of the monks flat on his face screaming in pain.

I ran to where he had fallen. He had twisted and broken his leg crossing small wooden bridge over a waterway to the kitchen. I recognized him immediately. He was one of the punk monks whom held me down in the ox pit. He looked at me in despair. I started walking away. I stopped as I heard his voice.

"Your name is Shiniwa. A forgiving sun".

I froze. I knew I could not leave him there. I thought I was alone in the monastery. Everybody had left to the lower edge of the prayers' mountain, as the climb was impossible. It was one of the very few days I had refused to join the others.

I walked back to him to survey his situation. I was a soccer player. I had seen players breaking their legs. I knew how dangerous it was to move someone with a broken leg without securing the injury.

I ran to the kitchen. I found a long board. I looked to strap his leg with something. There was nothing there. I lifted his leg and gently laid it on the wooden board. I tore my robe and secured his leg.

He was shivering. I ran back to my quarter to fetch a small blanket I covered myself at nights. I wrapped him tightly. I needed to get him out of that freezing cold. I found a wooden board we used as a tabletop in the kitchen. I pulled it off and slid it under the punk monk's body. It was easy to slide him over the snow-covered surface. I pulled him inside through the sleeping quarters. He was in a lot of pain. I could see his bone sticking out from the side of his knee.

I was not quite so sure what to do. I was astounded at my measures trying to leave him earlier in that sub-zero temperature and now I was hustling to help him.

Pain, that small river
Trembling the mighty ocean
Arrived in a little shoddy form
Then, ocean the majestic
Nobel was just a name.

"It is not important who you are. It is not how burly you shadow the earth. That you move so strong, the tallest tree looped knot. How you left the path, those who followed, that's who you are".

I sat by him. He was praying quietly. This is how these monks tolerated callously pain. He started to sing a song I had heard many times over:

> *Shall we yet, hold*
> *This, the day of peace*
> *Peace, my brother*
> *We fly to the sun*
> *Silently taking the cold*
> *The coldest touch*
> *Warmer the sun*
> *The burning sun*
> *I am home*
> *I am warm*
> *I am with the sun*

I had no idea what to do. I did not like him much but I could not just sit and watch him suffer. I could not understand how he could sustain that much pain in a clear sight. I ran to the library to look for any first aid book. I knew it was next to impossible.

"Miracles are the secrets within. Luck is the fool's gold".

> *Life is a great big canvas, and you should throw*
> *all the paint on it as you can.*

I returned to the injured monk who was now sitting against the corner of the wall. I was desperate and thwarted at finding nothing to help him. I sat next to him. Is there anything that I can do to alleviate your pain? I asked in a fainted voice.

Of course my friend. The monk sounded cheerful.

What? I asked.

"Sing with me Shiniwa. This pain will cease but this moment will stay for life". He said.

I did not know many of the words, but he patiently corrected me as we sat by the side of the cold sleeping quarter wall and sang that song which brought peace upon the soul of a wild and lonely boy.

He was not a philosopher. He was not a master or a mentor. He was just a simple monk who was so right. That moment lived forever.

I heard the others return. I jumped out to get help. I did not realize how quickly the time had passed by. The two older monks rushed to help the punk monk as I walked back to the lion head to continue my own version of meditation. I wanted to see, talk and feel the family I could not see anymore. The distant fog had dissipated.

"I am very proud of you. You are the shield of those broken. You are the lost promise in this forgotten mountain". I heard Kako as he held my shoulders from behind kissing my head.

I think that day I learned something priceless. That, how a simple human touch could lift an ugly scar.

"Live as if you were to die tomorrow.
Learn as if you were to live forever".

I was playing with my soccer ball a couple of weeks later when I heard the punk monk voice again. He was standing behind me leaning on two bamboo crutches. He passed a robe to me bowing.

I made this for you. He said. I looked at the robe. Mine had a big tear on the side when I used it to strap his leg. I bowed back accepting the robe graciously.

My name is Xione. I am very thankful for what you did for me. He leaned forward awkwardly reaching for my hands trying to knee. His face inundated with tears.

I am so miserable for what I did to you. I am . . . . He could not continue as he just sobbed.

What would you do if you had wings? Kako asked.
Silly question! I would fly. I barked back
What if, you had broken wings?

Angels had touched me and ecstasy had crowned me. I had no more urge to kick his ribs or break his head. I kneed holding him sobbing. I had nothing to say. I made peace with myself. I realized how good it felt to hold another person's hands feeling humble. I learned the meaning of ignorance through the hard way.

My eagle wings had folded exhausted.

I joined the group the next day for the walk to the prayer mountain.

"The grand essentials of happiness are: something to do,
something to love, and something to hope for".

It was not long that after one of those prayers' walks, I heard the gathering gong upon our return. It was quite unusual for the gong operator to play the gathering call that early in the morning. We all had many churns during the mornings, as the days were very short. We all walked to the shrine temple.

Master Ouiyen waved at me to sit by him. That was the most unusual. I was not considered a monk. I was an outlaw and a health hazard to many of those monks. Kako was standing smiling behind master Ouiyen.

I felt more comfortable seeing him there. I always felt uneasy being in that shrine. It felt creepy. Idols, relics and other such objects associated with the figure being venerated. There were votive offerings in the altar.

I walked cautiously to where master Ouiyen was. Master Ouiyen took my hand and invited me to sit next to him.

The gong operator played. The shrine went dead silent.

If you have love in your life, it can make up for a great many things you lack. If you do not have it, no matter what else there is, it is not enough. Master Ouiyen said.

According to Buddhist practice, there are three stages or steps. The initial stage is to reduce attachment towards life. The second stage is the elimination of desire and attachment to this Samsara. Then in the third stage, self-cherishing is eliminated. Master Ouiyen quoted HH Dalai Lama.

Shiniwa has taken the time needed in developing his spiritual practice. Once he understood the values of the teachings and felt they were appropriate for his own spiritual development, he took the next step to formally establish himself as an ordinate monk by taking "refuge". Here, we all have taken refuge and precepts through our lives without the rules of outside monks. Although, no matter, we have dedicated our being to our cause. I want you all to acknowledge your devotions and full attentions to our new football player monk. He is our joy and our pain. After all, he is Shiniwa, the Burning Sun. Master Ouiyen continued.

I was simply overwhelmed. Every monk was chanting.

CHAPTER NINETEEN

TRAINING

What extend you find delight and mirth,
Where there is burning without end?
In deepest darkness you are wrapped!
Why do you not seek for the light?
Look at this puppet here, well rigged,
A heap of many sores, piled up,
Diseased, and full of greediness,
Unstable, and impermanent!
Devoured by old age is this frame,
A prey of sickness, weak and frail;
To pieces breaks this putrid body,
All life must truly end in death.
Buddha

TRAINING SESSIONS WERE NOTHING OF WHAT YOU SEE in the Hollywood movies. They are pictorial tricks for an actor who suddenly suit a superman soaring in the air killing a group of thirty people using some visualized moves.

There was generally a great tension of nerves while my trainings were going on.

Though the wisdom of such institution was sometimes challenging, there was no doubt about its immense benefits. It was a good practical mind discipline.

That the so-called meditation practiced in our training is not the same mental training as it generally known in the West. As so much psychic energy is concentrated on the inner soul and lifting up your body above your physics, the physical side of our exercise underwent a great pressure to a point the entire body muscles became taut. Kako used to hit me with a stick to relieve the pressure. It was also to prevent me falling asleep.

The truth about those unsympathetic mind trainings somehow preserved in the midst of my prosaic flatness and shallow sensationalism of my western life.

"Only an intelligent eye detects a blade of grass to power transcending the vicissitudes of human life".

My training ultimate aim was to show the way to complete liberation from my personal sufferings by the attainment of an unconditioned state beyond the range of the normal untrained mind. Its immediate aim was to strike at the roots of belligerent suffering and humilities I sustained.

The innermost hub of every move in training was not only an unchanging soul but rather a life-current, an ever-changing stream of vigor, which was never the same for two consecutive seconds. The self, measured as an eternal soul, therefore, is a delusion, and when regarded from the ultimate standpoint it has no reality; and it is only within this delusion of selfhood, that eventual suffering can exist. When the self-delusion is finally transcended and the final illumination is attained, the ultimate state, which lies beyond the comparative universe, is reached. In this ultimate affirm, the unconditioned suffering is extinguished; but while any element of selfhood remnants, even though it is a delusion, suffering remains potentially within it.

Our training was at the corner of the first hill lead budding the monastery. You could see the giant walls hiding the prayer mountain behind them. It was a great place to watch the sunset every afternoon if you were not blown away with the cold and cruel wind. Sometimes the strong wind would make hiking up to the monastery very defiant. We had to crawl up as walking was punishable with soaring snow or frozen ice right into our face so strong to knock us flat on our back.

Sunset had different colors there. It felt as if sun was apologizing for leaving, extending into an unknown space to reach us.

It was a breeze once we had arrived at the first hill. There, GOD sat with his heavenly trays of unparallel sights. The northern lights envied the sun reflections over gargantuan mountains fresh snow.

"Sit down and fold your legs". Kako said.

I did.

Lift your body up pushing your fists against your weight. Kako said.

I tried my best with no success. I thought my legs were much stronger that my arms.

The wind was a big factor. My body was like a small twig against the power of a bulldozer pushing me down.

I kept on trying while he looked into the distance with his back to me.

What I am doing wrong? I asked.

There was no answer. Kako just looked into the empty space.

I kept at it and failed more miserably.

I was losing my patience.

I always wondered why his ways of tutoring were so strange. However, I had come to the terms of accepting them without questioning him or challenging his ways. I had learnt that I would lose.

"Put the wind behind you". Kako suddenly said. "Ride upon what comes to you as a hardship where it is only a clue. You are falling because you are fighting with your balancing whilst the wind pushing against you. Think of how to balance using the wind".

That evening I tried so hard that my knuckles were bleeding.

Once we arrived at the monastery, Kako held my hands inviting me to sit next to him.

"You do not need my help with every single problem. Rather, you should analyze your matters theologically. You could balance on your arms later with more practice. However, that is a circus act.

You must ponder on what the logics are, not the circus act of walking on your hands". Kako said.

I took a long time for me to manage to lift my body on my arms after I stopped thinking about just lifting. I used to close my eyes listening to the wind while twisting away from it. I think I found the focal point of the wind to sit on whilst lifting my body. I just stopped trying the circus act.

There were so many other maneuvers that Kako demand and I had to master.

Kneeing on one leg, facing the harsh wind for a long time without blinking, walking down the hill with my eyes shut and the master of all:

"Find me two identical rocks from the riverbed". Kako said pointing to the river one early autumn morning. "They must match perfectly and keep your eyes closed".

I do not think if there is anything in this world, more odd than looking for a pair of identical rocks from the riverbed with shut eyes. It was early autumn. The river water was ice cold.

I made many trips to the riverbed, freezing.

I never found what I was looking for.

I failed to see the logic behind it, as it was simpler that I could understand.

"Human perfect eyes are different from each other".

I did not find the matching rocks, but I found a great easy way of humiliation.

There was no need for perfection. However, those trips to the riverbed made perfect point.

CHAPTER TWENTY

MY PERSONAL SOCRATES

KAKO SELDOM DEMONSTRATED EXCITEMENT underneath his usual serious mien, though by this time I could read him pretty well. One day he allowed his excitement to show through as he said to me, "Shiniwa, we're going on a trip tomorrow! We're going to see some new places!"

I shouted for joy, "Yea!"

Very early the next morning, Kako woke me and we started off well before sunrise. I will never forget the crisp breeze of that summer morning, the freshness of the outdoors as we walked for quite some time. Kako, as was his custom, sang while I horsed around like a typical fourteen-year-old boy without a care in the world.

"What does that song mean?" I asked when he finished.

"It's about a small boy with a great soul," Kako replied, "He is a survivor, a traveler to unknown places. He saves many people and he is an artist with magical feet. He is the sun."

We talked about our ages, and Kako mentioned that from his best calculations he was now forty years old. Once Kako had told me that he would die at the age of forty-four. It all had to do with some Chinese mumbo-jumbo (at least that is how it appeared to me) about being born on the fourth day of the fourth month in such and such a Chinese year. While I was beginning to understand some of the wisdom of Kako's teaching, things esoteric made little impression on me. What was beginning to sink in, I put together in a kind of poem (or was it a mantra?)

Life is given. Life is the
most valuable gift shared
amongst the most gifted.
Trust your shadow, as
your shadow is your soul
Soul knows no devil. My
soul lived within my
brown, ragged robe. I
was a monk who didn't
know.

I have no idea if I had ever heard of the Greek philosopher/ teacher, Socrates. Certainly I have no idea if Kako knew anything about ancient Greek history. Today I understand that Kako's teaching method was much the same as the Socratic Method, raising questions for the student to formulate answers. I continued asking questions as he patiently guided me into discovery.

"What do you call that tree?"

"What are those green box looking shrubs?"

"Are we going to get lost here?"

The trees were so thick we had to push our way through them. They were arched, creating the most beautiful canopies, and we could hear so many birds in a wild chorus that was unbelievable and almost deafening. I was fascinated by everything we were seeing on this outing. In an open area, I saw the tallest tree I had ever seen in my life. I ran toward it.

"What is the name of this tree?" I asked.

No answer! Turning around, I did not see him.

"Hello, Kako, where are you?" Silence. "Are you hiding? Where are you?" I yelled as loud as I could, but my voice was swept away with the noise of the jungle birds. Nevertheless, I kept on yelling. But Kako did not answer.

I was lost in a forest. I had no clue where I was or what to do. Was this another of Kako's object lessons? I started to panic. I yelled again. Think Shiniwa. Think, he cannot be far way. But, why isn't he answering? I kept on shouting. I tried to backtrack. Everything looked the same. There were no footprints. What if I don't find him? I was hungry and scared. I can find my way, I kept telling myself. "Jiaoshi (master), where are you?" I had never before called him by that name. Suddenly something grabbed my shoulder from behind. I screamed so loud, scared to death.

It was Kako, my Jiaoshi with a red face and tomato colored lips.

"Where were you? You look like beets." I demanded.

He smiled, showing me some raspberry looking berries. Using sign language, he got it across to me that he had lost his voice from eating those juicy berries.

"Do you want to go back?" I asked.

He shook his head no. We had come to see that place and we were not leaving. That night we camped out with Kako using gestures and hand signals, a secret between the two of us that we laughed about for a long time. The place was amazing, a magical forest of natural beauty; and we were the only two humans inside that pristine wonderland that was a heaven mere miles outside the monastery where I had a hellish life. I took many more trips to that forest where that tall tree had replaced the apple tree.

"What do you do if you are lost?" Kako asked me later.

"Well, asking directions from the monkeys is out of questions. You couldn't talk to them, so I'd just scream," I said sarcastically.

"You will be strong. You shall search within. You dig deep within your knowledge and logical reasoning for what you know and ask questions. Fear is not an option. Yell, but hear yourself and listen," my master said.

Kako talked and taught me for many years. I listened and repeated. I was his favorite student. Kako was a self-taught man with the greatest wisdom, a man of principles and integrity a teacher and a master who held the highest degree from the University of Life. He was a scholar from an old world unknown to most people in what we call our modern civilization. To sum him up, Kako was a knowledgeable man who spent all his days reading and praying.

As I said, the arcane never really appealed to me, though I saw Kako do many things for which there is no book rational explanation. The idea of mind reading was one of those concepts I considered to be fantasy fiction; that is until I became Kako's student. There were times when he would put his hand on my shoulder and look me directly in the eyes as though penetrating my soul. He would smile and say, "Let it go, Shiniwa." Whenever I would complain (which was frequently), he would tell me that he knew what I was really thinking.

I was deep in thought one afternoon when I felt his presence again.

"Shiniwa, remember the time you switched your father's bottle with your urine? It is over son. You need to look ahead and let go.

Your anger at your father is tearing you to pieces. You may never see him again. It does not rain in a cloudless day," he said.

He was right. I was there nursing my hatred for my father even though I was in complete denial.

"You are spooky!" I told him.

He lowered his head with his hands crossed across his flat belly looking deep down as if there were something there and he was the only one who could see it. At the time, I was unaware of getting an education in spirituality along with my regular academic studies.

The beginning of my education in astronomy began with one of Kako's questions, "Shiniwa, why is the sky blue?"

The imp in me wanted to say, "Because God ran out of paint," but I knew better than to give such an answer. So I debated the question for hours, arriving at a conclusion that had a scientific foundation. Kako talked for what seemed like hours about the universe, teaching me everything he knew about astronomy, space, stars, and the galaxies. That night he had me look up and observe the North Star, planets, constellations, nebulas, and much more of a subject that I found as fascinating as mathematics. There in the Himalayas, without ambient light of any kind, viewing the stars was a vivid experience the likes of which I have experienced nowhere else on earth.

What I was getting in the way of education in my school under the sun by day and the stars by night was more than just the knowledge of science and language. Kako was giving me a hefty dose of philosophy in his clever way of getting me to use my brain. Kako never questioned my integrity nor expressed any doubts about me. He gave what he could give; and, most importantly, he gave me his unconditional unselfish love and passions—regardless of how cruel a recipient I was. It all came down to the reality that I was all he had and he was my world that I knew and owned. Looking back, I realize that the

Socratic style education I received at the monastery was far superior to anything I had ever gotten out of an eleemosynary institution.

Private schools had never really taught me to think the way I learned from Kako. I contemplated many things most people might say are beyond the ken of a normal pre-adolescent. I thought about the difference between imagination and reality. I contemplated the taste of life—is it like a fruit? If so, what fruit is it? Then I considered how often the simplest questions often go unanswered. I never thought of any question I raised as being so difficult that no one could answer.

Not everything in the monastery was all chores, and prayers, and lessons—at least, not after my arrival in the otherwise dismal place. Game days were the grant days. They were my most joyful days. I was the grand master, the marshal, and the executive officer. Those days belonged to me. I had the entire monastery under my feet.

I had the players, the audience, and the cheerleaders. I was the color commentator. I had them all. I chose who played and who was benched. I coached and I refereed. (After all it was my ball that Kako had made with an old coconut shell and strapped with bamboo strings.) Everybody was a patron and nobody was exempt.

Erzifo was always on my side and safe. Once the ball was out, it was my monarchy and I was the king. I enjoyed my kingdom. I was never fair. I was never right. I was only the king.

I divided the players into three groups where each group had four players. The middle group had to defend the ball from passing through the mid-field. It had to neutralize the offence by passing it to the other group. I was always in the middle maneuvering the ball to whomever I wanted to have it. It was my game.

Games, however, were secondary to the education I was receiving from Kako—an education of both my mind and my emotions, the latter of which was Kako's greatest challenge. It was, as I look back on the entire experience, and incredible juxtaposition of innocence and naivety, with Kako being the pure, uncomplicated mind directing me, the boy who had never seen anything in shades other than stark black and white. With absolutely nothing in common, Kako and I formed a relationship that was hand in glove in its closeness and fulfillment for each of us. He was a kind, simple man in search of answers to his uncomplicated life and I was a little boy looking for shelter. I was a gypsy in search of new places with no place to go. He was a teacher who wanted to teach, and I was the student who didn't know what to learn.

It took years before those lessons taught and memorized began to fall in place for me. Kako had made every corner a classroom and every rock a place to sit. He talked and I just listened. The language barrier gave way gradually to a communication where matter and substance could be examined, ideas exchanged, and lessons well understood. He made me write everything he said, and I had to memorize every page.

One day that I recall vividly, we were outside the monastery when we were caught by a thundershower. It was cold with a furious wind where we sought refuge from the elements by a large pile of rocks. Darkness was descending on us and I was freezing and hungry. To me it was consummate misery; to Kako, it was a teachable moment.

"Look through the rain and tell me what you see," he said.

I wasn't sure what to look for.

"Shiniwa, you don't have to look for anything in particular," he prompted.

I could see nothing, and I had a hard time keeping my eyes open through the cold rain and vicious wind.

"Shiniwa, rain is coming in a pattern which shapes pictures of a new life as it forms. It is in circles. It pours in lines and it flies close to your eyes. How can you see though it with your eyes closed?" he asked.

I forced my eyes open.

"Separate every drop and every line. Put a circle around it when it hits the rock. Put the lines together," he instructed.

I tried and I did not see anything. I even tried to put a circle around the ones hitting the rocks. Typically, I wanted to be able to do whatever Kako could do, but on this occasion it was hopeless. After that day, he spent countless hours and days teaching me when it rained. It took me years to figure out what he was telling me that rainy afternoon. When it finally became clear to me in my later life, it felt like a precious jewel around my neck.

CHAPTER TWENTY-ONE

LINGERING PAIN

THE PATTERNS OF MY LIFE MAY HAVE BEEN UNDERGOING a transformation that I was unaware of, but the residue of my past life lingered on. I was the mighty lion, the burning sun. I was named Shiniwa, but one night I had a terrifying dream so scary that I continued screaming way after I was awakened by Kako. In the dream I saw my sister with her arm dangling around her and my father with red spikes on his head waving a knife at her. It was so vividly real that Kako had to hold me in his arms to calm me down. There was no way I could go back to sleep for the entire night, but he didn't let go of me. He sang the story of birds that traveled to the sea to see the humpbacks and the green islands. Although I was very tired the next day, Kako began his most precious teachings of a different philosophy. This new instruction taught me how to dream.

"What was your dream?" He asked.

I told him. I hated my father. I could not stop shaking from the rage that was built up in me. I wanted him dead. I wanted him out my dreams and my life. I wanted to go and see my sister. I wanted to go back to school walking with Shahla along Thames. I missed Hailie.

It took Kako years to teach me how to dream of what I wanted to dream. When I finally mastered the technique, I was able to dream of my sister and talk to her. I could hold her hand and walk with her to school. I could sit in my old classroom looking at Hailie, winking at her. I found that I could not remember my mother, but I sat on my grandmother's lap playing with her rough hands and looking into her blue eyes.

There came a time when in my dreams I was even able to put my father in a graveyard. That was something that I was not allowed to do. Kako had strictly forbidden that, but I did it anyway.

How can you hate love?

Along the way, I discovered the gates to the souls of others. I found the wings that only angels had, and I wore them in my dreams. I flew over the land, but for all my fanciful dreams I was still lost. I believed a prisoner had the right to freedom once he had paid for his crimes. Although it was at least my sixth year in the monastery, there was no release or parole in store for me. I was held prisoner by some people who truly cared for me but didn't know how to set me free.

Mine was a prison without walls and no access to the outside world on a road that led to nowhere. There were no guards and no arms. There were no sniffing dogs or shakedown crews. They were just some bald-headed, half naked monks wrapped in brown who hardly spoke any words and, if they did, I could hear very little of what they said. I remembered what Kako had tried to teach me, that we are shaped by our thoughts; we become what we think. When the mind is pure, joy follows like a shadow that never leaves. My circumstances produced an inner conflict that was wearing down the deep-seated anger, rage, and hatred that had comprised most of my young life up to that point. It is a strange predicament. I was so full of hate, but I could not hate those kindly monks even if I so deeply wanted to. The monks were so innocent and so full of love. I began to have thoughts like these: "What is the appropriate behavior for a man in the midst of this world, where each person is clinging to his piece of debris? What's the proper salutation between people as they pass each other in this world of debris?"

In a very real way, we were all prisoners of a given moment. I was just a little boy who missed being a little boy. I was the same kid who would have my whole class cheering when I substituted the blackboard chalk with a piece of soap. I was the little imp who used a safety pin to attach the school uniform skirts of unsuspecting little girls sitting next to each other. I was the same player who led my little league soccer team to championship. I was the daredevil who changed the marks on my classmates' test papers. I was that kid—only now I was wearing a piece of brown cloth instead of a blue tailored, white colored jacket. I was now the kid who is always cold with a running nose as a sign of chronic bronchitis.

Here there was no principal to make fun of; rather an old monk who was the master and the leader of these simple men, Ouiyen the respected teacher. The taciturn monks would sit around the big wooden table in complete silence for many hours. Sometimes days would go by before I would hear one of them say anything. They always looked down while walking without exchanging more than a simple word to each other. They attended to their daily chores without asking for any help or having any expectations. It felt like their silent world was filled with words unknown to the outside.

The monastery was a scholarly teaching institute. Every monk would pass their daily knowledge to the others during the evening gatherings. There were sometimes some hot discussions about the Chinese occupation of Tibet.

I was the last outsider the monastery had accepted and over the years, I learnt that there were no newcomers to the monastery. I was the last.

Kako admitted that due to proximity of our monastery to the Chinese occupied areas and that master Ouiyen fear of political and atrocity of the outside world had forced him to believe that we were the last living pyramids of that monastery.

This was the world I had to share in my irrational and disrespectful way. There was no safety and no one was safe. "We all go through life as given (as Kako often told me). There is no knowing what will happen, even with all our expectations. But, what if life expires just as you knew what to expect, as though it never happened?" I thought. I wondered if I would ever have had thoughts such these had it not been for the way Kako was opening up my mind.

It was not long before Ouiyen announced that we were to go back to Iuery, a trip that was a long, boring hike but still somehow exciting. There were a lot of books there that we could use. The monks would make no preparation for the trip, just walk to the front of the monastery, wait silently for everyone else to join and the long walking journey would start. It was a late summer day, and Erzifo had left that day to the praying path, the mountain to the east of the monastery where we all would walk almost every day as part of our silent meditation and cleansing of our thoughts.

It was an uphill path to the summit of the prayer mountain which took a few hours to make the round trip. The path traveled through jagged edged rocks and lush green forests. Here was the home of the golden monkeys, passing through smaller cold summertime rivers with the monkeys flying overhead, jumping from one tree to another screaming. Erzifo had to stay behind with two other monks. I really wanted him to go with us but the decision was not his, he had to stay behind upon his arrival from the prayer pass. The rest of us set out on our little pilgrimage which took three long walking days. But Iuery was the only contact we had with the outside world and we all welcomed seeing new faces. Going there was like finding new life and seeing new lights.

Iuery monastery monks were trying their best to comfort us and keep us entertained but I missed my friend. Kako, knowing how much I wanted to have Erzifo with me, tried to keep me occupied as much as he could. I had made a ball for these other monks the last time we visited them and now they had their players and their team. It was a great opportunity for all of us to jump in the open space and play, something that we had all talked about all year long and now it was the time.

Midday after we all had completed our chores, we all rushed to the field. Nobody would have missed that opportunity. Naturally, I was the leader and the coach of my team, and my well-trained monks knew what to do. We were as confident as we could be, for after all, winning meant new books that we could take home from Iuery monastery, but if we lost we had to leave some beads behind.

It was the funniest thing trying to play with these other long brown-robed monks who could not run or walk fast with their robes all wrapped around their bodies as they were playing while we were in our designer monks' jerseys. We had bandaged feet playing against the others who had no shoes. As we walked to the field, the other monks were indeed appalled. They could not believe what they were seeing and insisted on having us play with our original robes. All objections overruled, our master Ouiyen ordered the game to start. Our Iuery opponents could not believe how organized and thunderous we were. It was the easiest game to win. I was the leader and the coach, and this was my game.

On our way back, we all could not stop bragging about the game and how well we played. I was looking forward to see my friend Erzifo to tell him about the game and how much I missed him. Kako just listened and smiled.

CHAPTER TWENTY-TWO

I CALLED HIS NAME, BUT HE DID NOT ANSWER

I FLEW THROUGH THE ENTRY GATE ONCE WE ARRIVED back at our monastery. I rushed to the corner where Erzifo and I called our room and suddenly froze in my tracks. My friend was on the floor attended by two monks. His head was all bandaged and his face was swollen and cut in many places. Both of his legs were wrapped.

I felt my whole body freeze. I stuttered and shook. I was completely paralyzed. I was in so much pain, my head started to spin. I could hear my heart pounding. My eyes went dark. I dragged myself to his side, grabbing him crying uncontrollably. I kept on calling his name but he would not answer. I learned that he had slipped over the rocks and fallen down the backside of the prayer mountain the day we left for Iuery. It had taken the other two monks a day to find him. He was unconscious and had lost a lot of blood.

Later that day we sent Erzifo on a small wagon to the nearest hospital which was three days away. Ouiyen did not allow me to accompany my friend to the hospital. I was gravely agitated. Kako held me tight, sharing my tears as my friend disappeared over the horizon. I had to stay behind.

My world and everybody else's had stopped. The silence was deafening, nobody would dare to say anything. We all just waited. Kako and I sat by the road, staring and praying, where the small wagon had taken Erzifo away. We did not move. The other monks would bring food for us and sit behind us. Then we all waited.

Two weeks passed. It was late that day when we could see the wagon in the distance. I started to run toward it as fast as I could, almost running into the ox as I was trying to climb onto the wagon. The companion monks jumped to their feet trying to stop me. I did not see my friend but there was a bandaged roll on the side of the wagon. One of the monks kneeled at my feet and held my legs. The monk was crying as he said my friend was dead. They had brought his body in that roll of bandage.

My world just ended. I lost my sister and never saw her again when I was in a soccer tournament; and now I lost the only friend I had while I was in another damn soccer game. That's not fair. Erzifo was fifteen. So was Shahla. What on the earth was it with my game and age fifteen? Kako tried to calm me down, but he, too, was in so much pain that he had to kneel down.

My pain was a dangerous anger known to all these people who had tried to bring peace to me in the last six years. It all ended that afternoon. I broke everything that was around me. I punched every tree and every wall. I kicked every corner that I could kick. I broke all of my knuckles. I imprisoned myself in the same corral with the ox, screaming, cursing, and crying. I had lost my friend the same way I had lost my sister. The only sound was my angry voice which traveled as far as it could with the entire monastery sharing a grief they had never experienced.

I don't know how long I lived in that corral. I did not eat or leave the corral. Vaguely, I heard Kako. He was standing in front of me.

"Shiniwa, we have to free Erzifo's soul. We have to let him go. He would have done the same for you," he said plaintively. I lit the fire where the body of my friend rested, and I gathered his ashes to bury under the apple tree.

His ashes brought a new peace to me but his absence was maddening.

Shahla died armless, Erzifo died legless from gangrene and I was still living to mourn them both.

Life is not about fairness, it is given and it is how
you process your time through it that is your life.

Erzifo was the angel whom my sister had sent to me and Kako was the guardian who cared for me as no other. My old bald man was the angel who came to my life sent by no one except life itself.

Kako was my new partner. He sat by me and sang the old songs and the new songs, the ones he sang to me when he used to put me to sleep. I slept on Erzifo's pallet and wore his robe. I held his flute. It was all he had. I guess that was a turning moment when I started to play his flute and I heard the entire monastery singing and clapping to the song Erzifo sang. They did this all afternoon that day as I played his flute. I made peace with Erzifo by living his life through his flute.

As for the monks, they were the same gentle men whose limbs I had broken and whose flesh I had cut, but they never stopped loving me. Vicariously, they were living my life now. But life in the monastery was never the same without Erzifo and his big cheerful laugh. Kako never left my side. He had dedicated his life to me; and now, with my friend's death, he was trying to cover for both. He was always the father I never had, the mentor who calmed the devil in me, and Erzifo had been my faithful friend and servant. Kako never stopped his teachings, but he did stop talking about Erzifo.

I was becoming quite domesticated by life in the monastery, and finally I was becoming more and more part of the group of the men who hardly spoke, but their many voices were heard. Although I was very skeptical, I even started to practice Buddhism. I got involved in many of the normal day to day prayers.

After so long a time, the monks were now comfortable around me, happy to teach me the old secrets of the religion. There were moments when I felt I was among my own family, and these monks were my own brothers. Nevertheless, there was always some resistance within me.

Kako, whose presence in my life had changed my character, always protected me and never even for once left me. He was sleeping where Erzifo used to sleep even though he had his own semi-private corner. Never before nor since have I witnessed such devotion bestowed on another human being.

I lost interest in my ball. I did not want to touch it again. I had kicked it somewhere the night of my outrage and that was the last time I had seen it. "Shiniwa!" Kako was there with the ball in his hands, "This ball has changed the life of every man in this place, don't let it die. I want you to go out and play. I need to see you with the ball."

I looked at him gravely. Suddenly I remembered the day Erzifo wanted to be my friend. He wanted to play. I had been unable to turn him down then, and I could not turn Kako down now. I walked with my ball in hand and saw all the monks in their game jerseys cheering as I walked to them. The game was on. The game was my life which I shared with a bunch of brown-robed monks who brightened their simple lives in the pleasure of chasing a silly ball. We were comrades whose lives had collided to form what we learned as students and as monks.

CHAPTER TWENTY-THREE

BURIED ALIVE

EVERY EVENING, AFTER THE NORMAL SIMPLE SUPPER, we were all inside the biggest section of the monastery where all the books were kept. It was like a library but we used it for all kinds of gatherings. I discovered that almost all of the monks were unfamiliar with outside world, and this small place with its evening gatherings and those books were the only contacts most of them ever had with that world. We were gathered together on one such occasion when the next major turning point came in my life.

We heard a roaring sound like hundreds of bulldozers driving by the monastery. Unsure of what the sound was, we looked at each other inquisitively. A couple of monks started to walk outside when there came the huge sound of a crash and the entire place rumbled. All the candles went out. We were suddenly chilled by a tremendous flow of icy air all around us. It was pitch dark. I could hear screaming and moaning.

I started to panic.

I called, "Kako!" There was no answer. I kept on calling him, and I felt snow all around me, so thick it was hard to move. There are no words to describe how cold it was. But worse than that was the frozen silence all around me in the dark. I wanted to scream but no sound came out of my mouth. I was shivering cold—so cold I could not feel my body. To this day I am not sure if it was fear or the atmosphere that chilled me so.

"What do you do if you are lost? Let's say it's a dark forest like where the monkeys are!" Kako once asked me.

Flippantly I had answered, "Well, I suppose asking directions from the monkeys is out of the question."

"You will be strong," Kako went on, ignoring my irreverence. "You shall search within and reason logically. Fear is not an option."

I remembered those words as I was standing motionless waste deep in snow. I am not lost! I thought, I am just . . . . I did not know what I was!

"Shiniwa! Shiniwa, where are you?" I heard Kako calling me and I knew I was safe.

"Talk to me, son, where are you?" I heard Kako again.

"I am here. I am here!" I screamed, "I'm stuck in snow. I can't see anything!"

I felt a hand over my face. "Your face is all frozen Shiniwa!" Kako said cleaning snow from my eyes. I could hardly see his face, but I knew he was there. You are so ugly! I thought irrationally. He had an angel face. Were you born with your legs first? I used to joke with Kako and he was always so gracious. I never before knew how dependant on him I was, but I was too proud to admit to it. After all, I was Shiniwa, the burning sun.

There was a jumble of Kako's teachings rattling around in my disoriented brain. I could almost hear him saying, "The Sun goes to rest at night and shines new life the next morning!"

"It's an excuse!" I had exclaimed.

"It might be, but the Sun does not complain. It is explicit and free. Just like your soul. You can't stop either of them as they both are the same."

"I am cold," I said.

Kako pulled his robe off to wrap around me. His body was naked and snow covered. I did not dare to ask him if he was cold or freezing. I think I was so selfishly arrogant that I only mattered at that moment.

"Help me, Shiniwa, look for others. I know you are cold." Kako sounded desperate.

There were mountainous snowdrifts everywhere. The half moon above was like a bright light shining over the frigid, reflected landscape. Parts of monastery had disappeared. I found myself standing next to Kako, protected by the library wall with the roof gone.

"What happened?" I asked.

"Shiniwa, look for others, move son!"

I gathered all the strength I had. I knew at that perilous moment that there was no time to be a child anymore. I had to act as the captain of the team to save my players. Kako was scrambling to find ways to move around the deepest snowdrifts when I saw something hanging from the wall. I remembered it was a large bamboo woven basket held by two old wooden paddles. I struggled toward it, jumping through the cold snow. Somehow I grabbed and pulled the basket down. I stepped inside the basket and used the paddles to move around.

It was a difficult task but it was a lot easier to move with the basket.

I pulled alongside Kako. "Give me the paddles!" he demanded.

He put the paddles on the top of the snow using them as steps while pulling me behind. It was deadly quiet.

"Where is everybody?" I asked when suddenly my basket moved up and I flew off to the side. I screamed. Then, I saw one of the monks standing where my basket use to be. He looked like a ghost, completely disoriented but unharmed and shivering. He grabbed my arms and pulled me toward him praying! Now, there was a group of three of us. We did not care how deep the snow was, we just moved around searching and yelling.

Another of Kako's teachings came unbidden into my mind. "If you're wishing for something, what do you do?" I had asked Kako.

"Turn the wish into a picture, and look at it as often as you can, until you can paint it in your dreams."

I wish I could find everybody, I told myself, but where are they? Sunk in this frozen snow, there was no time to dream or learn to paint it in my dreams.

I heard some commotion behind me. Kako had spotted two more monks who were pinned against the wall. It took very little effort to free them, both so thankful but obedient to Kako's orders to search for others. It felt like an endless search but more and more monks were showing up once we moved to look around the broken walls.

We all had frostbite, but that did not matter. We just swept around, digging into the snow with bare hands. The monks were singing prayers as they were digging. I imagined that sound as melting the snow:

I share my life with you.
I warmed my heart with you.
I hungered with you.
I feasted with you.
I flew borrowing your wings.
I sailed with your waves.

> *We are brothers.*
> *We traveled life together.*

I heard one of the monks screaming for help and we all rushed towards him. It was then that we all saw our first dead brother monk. His peaceful face was so soothing as though he were kissing us farewell. His neck was crooked and his body totally bent.

Kako tried to calm down the monk who had found the dead brother. There were more people trapped.

"Please don't stop!" I screamed, not knowing how I found the strength to say that in that long night that was getting longer with no end in sight.

We found areas that were clear of snow where we carried the monks who were injured and could not help. It was a bloody cold shelter and not large enough for everybody, however, those fragile, innocent and shivering bodies of half-life monks were stronger than any Olympic Champions.

Haunting flashes of memory came to me like the time I shouted angrily, "I hate this place, I hate you, and I hate all of these monkey looking naked ass guys! Go and burn in hell." I kicked the tomato plant Kako cared for so tenderly.

That was then and now I was pushing as hard as I could to find the same monkey looking naked ass guys that I wanted to save. Now I wanted to find them and keep them warm.

I had always thought myself so superior; but in the aftermath of the avalanche, humility and despair were leaving deep marks and visible guilt. The moments of joy are rather short winning a championship, but the real pleasures in life are endless in their rewards. At the time, as I frantically searched with Kako and the other monks for any more signs of life, I was unaware of the transformation going on in my psyche. I was a candle burning brighter than city lights. In the process my spirit was rising to new heights as I shared what I never knew I had—the love and caring that Kako had planted in me during all those hard years.

The sun began rising lazily, helping us move around easier. We had located some more monks who had serious frostbite but they were alive. Still, however, we were missing a few monks, and as the sun rose, we saw at last the magnitude of the devastation. The avalanche had torn through the middle of the monastery and had ripped apart the walls. It was like a giant long white snake that had split our place in two. When there is nothing to lose, more tragedy does not hurt. We had lost everything in those four walls that were no longer a protective refuge; but more than that, we had lost some very good men.

By midday we were all accounted for with seven dead. We did not mourn as we set about to move our lost comrades within what was left of the kitchen and hallway. We needed shelter and the night was approaching fast, so we all worked together—even the ones who were injured. Nobody stood still. That was the code.

We managed to pull some bamboo poles together to build a small room covered by whatever we could find. As darkness pulled close, we all sat inside that poorly covered shelter, praying and sharing every piece of clothing we had to keep each other warm. It was a long and cold night. Many were injured but pain was secondary to those strong willed mountain warriors. The next day we cremated our dead brothers.

It looked as if nothing had really affected us, but we all mourned our fallen friends in our silent ways. It took a long time before we were able to start rebuilding our monastery, because the needed materials were covered under the snow. Normal life is taken for granted, but there was nothing normal about living on a mountaintop surrounded by bigger mountains in the vicious constant cold wind. It was like foreboding music played by an unknown symphony and heard by only a few. I thought of it as a cruel story with no end, a pageless book with no title.

There was nothing normal about it. Of course life on this mountaintop had never seemed normal to me; it had been something I could not let go of simply because to get away meant a long walk down the mountainside if luck was on my side.

The monks never stopped working. There was always something going on. We would get excited when we found more jungle wood to rebuild what was left of the monastery. It was us against wild nature offering very little, but surrender we did not, even though the monastery was always cold at that high elevation and extreme Himalayan temperature. The wind never stopped.

Now it was hard to climb down the side of the monastery to reach the flat platform where we farmed rice. The small river that we had named SHOG would turn to a raging flow in spring making access to the outside world impossible. None of us knew of the outside world or cared about the outside world. Our world was a hilltop fifteenth century abandoned fortress with a steep bordered road to it and some rice patties by its skirt.

CHAPTER TWENTY-FOUR

LIFE AND LESSONS GO ON

KAKO AND I GOT MUCH CLOSER AFTER ERZIFO'S DEATH and the snow avalanche. We were almost inseparable. He was my parent and my comrade and I was his son. His teachings took longer hours and our walks covered further distances. We took it upon ourselves to build new vegetable gardens and plant bonsai trees. We started new and excruciating exercises which occupied most of our days. He called it "The waves of spirit."

We sat next to each other at an angle facing away from each other, and he would make me balance on one knee while holding both arms stretched. It took me weeks before I mastered that position. At the beginning my body was so sore I could not sleep at nights but as time went by it became easier.

Once I felt comfortable with one position, there came the next step, not thinking of anything while my body was traumatized by its own weight. I did not dare to complain or say anything. My real training days had only just begun, and I knew it well. Kako would simply wave his hands, smiling, every time I fell down during any of those exercises.

There were times when Kako would disappear for hours. I thought that was odd since always before he was constantly within my vision.

He meditated daily, but it was always in the open fields surrounding the monastery. We both had favorite places to meditate, but my friend was becoming more and more absent and secretive. I would not dare to spy on him. It was not how he had trained me. However, as his absences got longer, I knew something was not right.

He was to talk about certain stars one evening, and I waited at ridge of the hill where his nightly classes were held. He would never miss my teachings, but on this night he was late. I was getting worried. I had started down toward the monastery to look for him when I saw a shadow of a man on the side of the dirt road. Running to see who it was, I found Kako kneeling as if in prayer. I grabbed his shoulder, looking at his face. What I saw was as though someone had stabbed a knife between my eyes. My master's face was in so much pain, and he was holding his chest with his teeth clinched. He couldn't talk.

I took Kako in my arms and ran toward the monastery. His body was burning. Once at the monastery, the older monks surrounded him, trying to help my mentor who was very sick. I sat by his bed helplessly. There was nothing I could do except pray. I held my friend's hand, sobbing. I did not want to think. I knew I would go insane if I let my thoughts travel through my past. I stayed positive, assuring myself that my master would be just fine.

The monks were like butterflies fluttering around in their attempts to cure whatever was afflicting Kako. Nobody held anything back or left the corners of the monastery where Kako and I were. I slept by his feet with my hand across his body while my friend slept in peace.

The monks were treating Kako with all the natural remedies available to them. It was a long and slow process. Much later, I was sleep when I felt a hand stroking my head, and I thought I was dreaming of Hailie when she used to comb her fingers through my hair. Suddenly, I knew I wasn't dreaming. Kako had taught me how to dream and that was not my dream. I jumped to my knees! Kako was sitting with two monks holding him upright.

"You always think about that pretty girl, don't you?" Kako said with a faint smile on his face.

I broke into tears, holding him tight. I didn't know what to say. Nothing else mattered. My master was back. Kako was sick for quite some time, but he never stopped teaching me even from his bedside. My training and the maneuvers I was introduced to took my education into the realm of the spiritual that was by far the most intense part of Kako's training.

I had to do things like track the movements of bees or flowers while maintaining a perfectly stationary position. Everything I tracked visually, I had to do by listening, memorizing, and rebuilding in a kind of homework that Kako would correct. The process of this kind of education mesmerized me, absorbing me in a kind of concentration I never knew I possessed. Kako would listen to my recitations while moving his fingers like a maestro conducting a symphony orchestra.

Kako never criticized. He only smiled and touched the beads he wore on his left wrist as he listened and spoke effectively in his beautiful, soft voice. He used stories to make his points filled with wisdom and a philosophy as old as time itself. The more difficult my assignments, the more interesting my lessons became, and I observed that this education I was getting from Kako was no soccer game with cheering fans that you would expect to pat you on your shoulder. More important than being able to control a ball on the playing field, my lessons were teaching me mind control and cleansing of the soul as I maintained strict physical positions. Every time I failed I had to start from the beginning which was no fun.

The maneuvers I was learning were like steps to climb, and if I had to repeat everything because of a failure, it might take the entire afternoon to complete. There was no glory or trophy in what I accomplished; rather, I felt an inner satisfaction that I could not share with anyone. I did not dare to brag about anything I had accomplished because Kako would stare at me like a hydrant over a matchstick fire.

CHAPTER TWENTY-FIVE

THE ENDING AND THE BEGINNING

IT WAS A COLD FALL DAY WHEN I WAS FINISHING MY afternoon training, standing on one toe with my body stretched outward and my hands crossed with my eyes closed.

Kako normally would call after a short period to finish that exercise and to open my eyes, but this time it seemed to go on forever. I was getting really tired and I knew I could not hold out much longer, but I was not allowed to talk unless spoken to.

My leg was getting sore and my thighs were tightening. Not knowing what to do, I held on, just waiting for Kako, not even daring to open my eyes.

Finally my leg gave way and I fell to the ground. I opened my eyes to see why I had to take that punishment. Kako was not there. He never failed to surprise me, but this was not his way. I called after him; there was no response. I never knew what he did while my eyes were closed during my trainings, but every time before when I opened my eyes he was always standing in front of me.

I called his name several times. He never answered. I sat there motionless meditating and waiting. I waited for as long as I could before I started packing our daily equipments that we took with us to the open field near the apple tree. As I was moving around, I saw

Kako. His head was thrown back with his mouth wide open. His face was white, and I knew instantly he was not asleep. I had never seen him sleep during the day, nor had I ever seen his face being so pale.

I ran to my mentor who seemed so lifeless, and I tried to shake him. He did not move. My heart stopped. I was not able to talk. All I did was grab the man I loved more than myself and started running toward the monastery. I did not know what to think. I just knew that I wanted someone to help me. I needed my mentor to talk to me again. My mind was racing. Kako was a big man, but that did not matter. I just ran faster holding my mentor in my arms.

Once I passed through the monastery main gate, my knees simply fell from underneath me. Other monks rushed to help. I just held Kako's hand, praying. This was no Erzifo. This was Kako, to me an immortal, my friend I thought would never die. They moved my mentor inside where every monk stood by the door in total silence. My crying was the only sound.

We had no doctor or medical supplies. Hardly anyone ever got sick in the monastery. If we felt under the weather, our standard remedy was a bowl of hot soup. Two of the oldest monks attended to Kako, but there wasn't much they could do. I heard a commotion outside the room where Kako lay as the monks started to move him. I jumped up like a wounded animal.

"What are you doing?" I screamed.

"We're sending Kako to the hospital. We don't know what to do here, Shiniwa."

The loyal ox and his carriage were outside. I lifted my mentor and carried him to the carriage, laying him on top of bales of hay. No one tried to stop me from going with him. I held Kako's head in my lap as the ox started to move with two other monks walking along side the cart.

My mind flashed back to random moments from our past as the ox cart lumbered along.

"Hey Kako, look what I found."

Kako rushed to where I was standing and holding a small yellow and red baby bird which apparently had fallen from its nest above. There was blood around his beak. Kako bent down and gently picked up the injured bird.

"Are you going to put him back in his nest?" I asked.

"No, Shiniwa, his mother has rejected him. That's why he's here."

"What do you mean? How could his mother reject this baby? It is just a bird." I said.

"Well, look at him; you see those red colors over his wings? That's why." Kako said.

"Are you saying his mother just threw him out because he has red-colored wings?"

"Yes, Shiniwa!" Kako said.

"So, what are we going to do with him?" I asked.

"You are going to be his mother and make him well!" Kako said.

"Oh, ok. But I don't know how to be a mother bird. What if he doesn't want to fly?"

Kako only smiled.

I was happy to have a baby bird pet. Kako and I made a wooden box from bamboo for Dookie Junior, but I called him DJ. That little bird became the talk of the usually silent monastery. Everybody would bring something to feed the little bird. DJ was like my soccer ball that everybody looked at and nobody dared to touch.

One day after noon, Kako called and asked me to take DJ with me. We walked outside toward the SHOG River running through the valley peacefully.

"Open DJ's cage door and let him go!" he said.

We both watched DJ as he flew to the first tree. I thought he chirped his thanks as he continued into the forest. I always thought he would come back one day, but I never saw DJ again. You can cage a body but not a spirit. DJ was the spirit bringing a short new life to a young life. The metaphor was not lost on me. I was a caged bird yearning to be free.

As the ox cart continued moving over the rough road through the night, I held my motionless last friend. Not really knowing how, I prayed, "God, I know you can hear me. Kako always says you are always next to my heart. So, if you can hear me, listen to this. Do you remember Dookie, my sister Shahla, and Erzifo? Kako says God has a way of sending messages. Well, I want to send you a message. God, please help Kako. I have nobody left. You took away everything and everybody. Kako says you are fair. Well, where is the fairness here? You know God, would you want to be in my place with nothing left? I don't know if I could be a better God than You, but I would not do what you are doing to me. It is not right, you know, God. I have been punished for years for just being me. How do you get punished? Kako says in a place of power, you must be humble and forgiving. God, will you be humble and forgiving? God, will you help me? Will you help my Kako?"

I cried uncontrollably as we rode through the cold of the night and the two monks pushed the ox and the carriage relentlessly. The monks did not speak or stop; they only pushed their way as hard as they could singing the prayers.

We, all shall sit next to the fire.
We, all shall cheer.
Fire will brighten our souls that we share.
Broken lives, no broken souls.
We touch; we cherish.
This is the soul of a tiger.
We are the shadows.
We shadow no souls.

It was mid sun. "Shiniwa, Shiniwa!" I heard my name. I jumped looking around. There were the monks, the ox, and my lifeless mentor. But who was calling? Who was calling? I started screaming, "Who is calling my name?"

The two monks were looking at me as if I were completely insane. But they said nothing. I did not know how to let go of all I had. My face was swollen and completely wet. I held Kako so tightly that one of the monks had to rescue him from my grip.

We kept on pushing the ox and the cart as we forced our way toward the place we knew we could find some medical help. We were overwhelmed by Kako's unconscious body. I knew he was not dead. I didn't want to believe that. The ox was dead tired, but we could not stop. Yet a few hours later, the ox balked. The poor animal could not walk anymore. It had been over a day that he was pulling the small wagon where we had Kako.

The road ahead was almost impossible to continue without the ox pulling the cart. We had to stop and let the poor animal rest. We pulled the harness off the ox to let him take his ease. The moon was shining over the endless valley. We could hear the golden monkeys and see the butterflies which were like millions of little sparks in the air. I wasn't very sure if Kako was breathing, but it didn't matter. I wished I could do something, but there was nothing I knew how to do. After a couple of hours, we tried to force the ox to get up, but the poor old creature didn't move. I kicked him over and over again just like those times when the monks put me in his pit. The ox just sat.

I was so frustrated. I did not know where to kick him anymore. One of the monks got between me and the beast.

"Shiniwa, he won't get up!"

"What do we do now?" I asked.

The monks were puzzled. We needed the ox.

"We are going the pull this wagon ourselves!" I said, and the monks did not blink. We offloaded everything and strapped ourselves to the wagon. As we moved along, we kept on falling and hitting ourselves against the rough road and the punishing rocks, but nothing mattered. When the road finally flattened, we decided to let one of us rest inside the wagon as the other two pulled. It was the most difficult task to do, but years of physical training were paying off. After sun rose over the hills, we found a villager who kindly loaned us an old mule to pull the cart.

Another day passed before we arrived at the small city where there was a small hospital. Two nurses rushed Kako inside a room while we waited outside. The monks and I were so exhausted and hungry that we all passed out. I almost jumped out of my skin when a nurse tried to wake me up.

"How is my friend?" I asked.

"You can come in," the nurse said.

I rushed in to the room where Kako was and saw him sleeping on a bed with all kinds of wires and tubes hooked to his body. His face was completely covered so that I could not see his eyes. I held his hands as hard as I could.

I intercepted a doctor who seemed to be too busy to talk to a young innocent looking monk who seemed like a nobody. He was wrong. He had to talk about Kako because I was Shiniwa. It did not take long for him to realize although I was wearing a monk's robe, I was one angry violent person. He told me they needed more tests and he could not really say more.

Kako was in a complete coma. I sat by him, held his hands, and rubbed his feet. Two days later the doctor pronounced him dead. Kako was 44, as he had predicted for his death. I lost my only attachment to this world. Kako had been my life raft in this rough ocean of life.

He was gone. The loss and sorrow of losing Kako deeply affected my mental and physical abilities. The monks sat me next to the covered body of Kako and started the endless ride back to the monastery. I could not cry or move at all. I just sat in that cart motionless next to Kako. Once we arrived back at the monastery, all I remember was that the monks cremated Kako while I sat like a child with autism, completely lost in a vague world.

PART V

SHINIWA

CHAPTER TWENTY-SIX

RISING FROM THE ASHES

THE LOSS OF KAKO WAS UNLIKE THE OTHER devastating departures in my life. The difference, of course, was the education I had received at my mentor's hands. Instead of rage and anger, with Kako's passing I went into a shock that literally paralyzed me. I could do nothing but sit and stare into the excruciating void that was my life. The monks were extremely kind. There were always two or more of them around me where I sat motionless staring. They were feeding me and putting me to bed. During daytime, they were holding me from under my arms trying to urge me to walk.

I had no desire to do anything anymore. I dreamed of my master, sitting with him under the apple tree. I walked with him alongside the narrow dirt road to SHOG. I fished with him, ate with him and laughed with him. I saw him pulling me out of the corral and cheering when I scored in a soccer game. In my dreams, I relived those times when we had made noise together to break the monastery's deafening silence.

For months I remained in that mental limbo until finally I felt stronger and was able to move around on my own power. Even then, however, I isolated myself from the rest. Instead of in dreams, I walked the paths I used to take with Kako to sit under the apple tree for hours and hours. I began practicing the same maneuvers my mentor had taught me. There were times when I did not return to the monastery for days, staying by the apple tree or the lake. Almost amusingly, I could feel the presence of the monks who were checking on me without getting too close.

Life is a treadmill. Lucky ones walk off.

The treadmill of my life went on and on—walking or running incessantly, but getting nowhere. I lacked the courage to step off, and the recurring nightmares and lack of sleep only aggravated the situation. Just before I completely fell to pieces, I experienced a strange dream that caused me to jump out of bed, sweating. Whatever that dream had been, it was the catalyst that got me off the treadmill and put new determination in my soul. The next morning, after the monks had returned to the monastery from their morning ritual, I went to see Ouiyen.

I told the old Master that I wanted to leave. I wanted to go back to England. The old monk, who was always quiet and walked around the monastery with the help of his bamboo cane, stared at me for a long time.

"I know, Shiniwa! He was in my dreams, too. I have already made the arrangements. I was waiting for you to ask!" the old man said. That statement left me with little doubt that Kako was still with me. I recalled his saying to me one time, "You will live in peoples' hearts and thoughts if you live a pure life." It was Kako's purity that was calling me back to life.

A month later I started walking back on the eight-day trip to the ferry seaport that I had taken eleven years earlier as a child. The journey then had set into motion all the elements that changed me from a child into the young, strong man I was now who needed to face a world I had left as a child. For eleven years I had seen no one except warrior monks in a world where time had stopped. Now I was ready to re-enter the world I had once left behind, fully prepared through Kako's teaching to deal with whatever awaited me as I moved confidently toward the ferry that would take me back to my starting point.

After his cremation, we had buried his ashes under the old apple tree as he had desired. Surreptitiously, I managed to take a small amount of those precious ashes so that I could have at least a part of Kako with me always. The clothes on my back, my journal with notes I had copied during my studies, and the priceless ashes were all the possessions I had in the world as I walked back toward a life that had abandoned me eleven years earlier.

This was not Michael returning. It was a teenager on the verge of full manhood, wearing a dingy and tattered once white robe. The figure hiking alone over the rocky terrain was Shiniwa, the burning, rising sun, looking for new horizons to face and conquer.